Goals for social integration and realities
of social exclusion in the Republic of Yemen

International Institute for Labour Studies
United Nations Development Programme

# Goals for social integration and realities of social exclusion in the Republic of Yemen

Mouna H. Hashem

with the collaboration of the Education
Research Development Centre

Research Series 105

# Research Series

The aim of the Research Series of the International Institute for Labour Studies is to publish monographs reflecting the results and findings of research projects carried out by the Institute and its networks. The Series will also occasionally include outside contributions. The monographs will be published in moderately priced limited offset editions. The Institute thus hopes to maintain a regular flow of high-quality documents related to its areas of continuing interest.

ISBN 92-9014-574-9

*First published 1996*

Copies of this publication can be ordered directly from: ILO Publications, International Labour Office, CH-1211 Geneva 22 (Switzerland).

## SOCIAL EXCLUSION AND DEVELOPMENT POLICY SERIES

The concept of social exclusion is now extensively used in policy debates in Western Europe to describe emerging patterns of social disadvantage, particularly associated with long-term unemployment. It is a complex notion which can be used to denote, on the one hand, a situation or process experienced by individuals, namely their marginalization from society through economic deprivation and social isolation; and on the other hand, a situation or process which occurs in societies, namely the fragmentation of social relations, the emergence of new dualisms, and the breakdown of social cohesion.

The concept focuses attention on the process, agency, and the multidimensionality of disadvantage. It provides a framework for analysing the relationships between livelihood, well-being and rights. And it offers a way of considering how the social institution of citizenship is changing as various social contracts, the welfare state with a commitment to full employment in the North, and various forms of developmentalist state in the South, break down.

This volume is part of the IILS Research Series on social exclusion and development policy. The first volumes in this series explore the relevance and value of the notion of social exclusion in a global context, including in: newly industrializing countries; least developed countries; and socialist countries in transition. All these monographs are based on primary research carried out by local multi-disciplinary teams which examined the analytical and policy advantages of viewing poverty, inequality and lack of employment from a social exclusion perspective. This work sought to fashion approaches to social exclusion which were not Eurocentric. It was embedded in a common general framework which gave maximum discretion and scope for new approaches and insights rather than standardized research questions and methodologies for comparative analysis.

These monographs are the product of the IILS/UNDP project "Patterns and causes of social exclusion and the design of policies to promote integration". Other publications from this project, also based on country case studies, are published in the IILS Discussion Paper Series. The project was initially directed by Gerry Rodgers, and then by José B. Figueiredo and Charles Gore. Opinions expressed in the monographs are not necessarily endorsed by the IILS, ILO, or UNDP.

José B. Figueiredo and Charles Gore
Series Editors
International Institute for Labour Studies

### Social exclusion from a welfare rights perspective in India
*by Paul Appasamy, S. Guhan, R. Hema, Manabi Majumdar and A. Vaidyanathan*

### Social exclusion and inequality in Peru
*by Adolfo Figueroa, Teofilo Altamirano and Denis Sulmont*

### Economic transition and social exclusion in Russia
*by Natalia Tchernina*

### Poverty and social exclusion in Tanzania
*by Frederick Kaijage and Anna Tibaijuka*

### Challenging social exclusion: Rights and livelihood in Thailand
*by Pasuk Phongpaichit, Sungsidh Piriyarangsanan and Nualnoi Treerat*

### Goals for social integration and realities of social exclusion in the Republic of Yemen
*by Mouna H. Hashem*

Copies can be obtained directly from ILO Publications, International Labour Office, CH-1211 Geneva 22 (Switzerland).

# *Preface*

Analysis of social exclusion comes at a particularly important time with the global changes taking place in political economies, technology, and population growth. Global divisions are no longer perceived along the axis of East-West but rather North-South. These changes have been accompanied by rising levels of unemployment, poverty and lack of social integration in many low-income countries of the South. Those not included in the economic development process are trapped in a cycle of deprivation, poverty and social exclusion.

Poverty has always been one of the major ailments of developing countries. Development policies in the last 40 years have experimented with different concepts and policies to alleviate poverty, enhance economic development and improve the quality of life of people in developing countries. The concept of social exclusion is a continuation of this experimental process.

This monograph analyses the process of social exclusion which is closely related to the notion of social integration in the Republic of Yemen. It is not intended to be a comprehensive and all-inclusive study but rather an effort to highlight the importance of integrating the concept of social exclusion in development policies that aim to provide effective anti-poverty and social integration strategies.

My sincere appreciation to the various staff of the ministries (Ministry of Planning and Development, Ministry of Insurance and Social Affairs, Ministry of Health, Ministry of Education, and Ministry of Agriculture) of the Republic of Yemen, the Social Organization for Family Development and the Tihama Development Authority for their time and assistance in this study. I would also like to acknowledge the numerous individuals from the defined "excluded groups" whose cooperation was crucial for the successful conduct of this study.

To Dr. Abbas Aidarous, Dr. Ibrahim Al-Houthy, Dr. Insaf Abdu Kasem, and all the ERDC investigators, many thanks for your efforts. This study would not have been possible without your participation. It was a pleasure and an honour to have the opportunity to work with you.

My gratitude to Dr. Gerry Rodgers for inviting me to participate in this project. Also, many thanks to Dr. Charles Gore for his valuable advice and insightful suggestions during the preparation of this monograph. There are many others, too numerous to name, who were of tremendous assistance in the conduct of this study. My heartfelt apologies for not being able to mention everyone by name.

Last, but not least, thanks to my very young travel companion, Rashid, for his patience and understanding during our many trips back and forth across the Atlantic while preparing for this study. I hope he will find it in his heart to forgive me for his "exclusion" from his rights to more fun and play with mom while I was busy researching social exclusion in Yemen! The opinions expressed in this monograph are solely those of the author.

Mouna H. Hashem, Ph.D.

**Participants from the Education Research Center, Sana'a, Republic of Yemen**

Research Director, ERDC, Dr. Ibrahim Al-Houthy
Technical Director, ERDC, Dr. Insaf Abdu Kasem

Investigators:

Dr. Ali Muhammed Almutaa'h
Ilham Kassem Abdu
Ahmad Ghaleb Mugbel Ad-Haboob
Ahmad Mohammad Gahlib Al-Kadazi
Ali Yahya Ahmad Al-Nuzaili
Hamud Abdulrahman Al-Kahtani
Khaled Muhammed Al-Dubani
Wahbia Abdulla Al-Hamami

Sultan Mohammad Saleh (ERDC Aden)

# Contents

# Introduction

Poverty is becoming more visible in Yemen. A growing number of Yemenis lack access to adequate housing, safe drinking water, health care services, education, income, or sufficient nutrition. Problems of poverty have become more widespread since the beginning of this decade as a consequence of a series of economic and political crises that have shaken the fragile infrastructure of the country. Hence, those that were already poor have become poorer and many who were not have since joined the ranks of the poor.

Social exclusion in Yemen is strongly associated with poverty and the marginalization of certain groups from the benefits of social and economic development. What distinguishes the poor from the excluded, however, is that the poor may still be within the mainstream of society. The excluded, on the other hand, are groups that have been pushed out into the periphery of society. They are not only deprived from basic goods and services but also lack social networks and effective political representation to assist them in reintegration. Thus, as the process of development proceeds, those who are left behind are trapped in a cycle of poverty and exclusion.

Identifying processes of social exclusion and, on this basis, promoting integration of excluded individuals and groups are critical for the country's success in attaining economic development. Until this is achieved, the country will continue to be pulled apart by two opposing dynamic forces: the efforts to transform the country into a modern market society, and the acute problems of poverty and poor mobilization of human and natural resources.

The problems of poverty and social exclusion are country-specific. This monograph aims to address the following questions:

1. What is the concept of social exclusion in Yemen?

2. What are the mechanisms that lead to exclusion?

3. What are the major dimensions of exclusion that are most prevalent in Yemen?

4.   Who are the most vulnerable to exclusion?

5.   What is the relationship between poverty and exclusion?

6.   What roles do social institutions and social actors (for example State, non-governmental organizations, international organizations) play in social exclusion and integration?

A central argument of the study is that the dual nature of Yemeni society gives rise to dual processes of exclusion. On the one hand, exclusionary practices arise in social relationships based on traditional cultural values of the social order. On the other hand, there are processes of exclusion related to the transformation of society to a modern economy state.

At the macro level, the monograph seeks to define the concept of social exclusion in a way that relates it to the rise of dualism and the particular nature of social integration in Yemen. This requires discussions of the political history, economic, and social context of Yemen. At the micro level, the objective is to explain the dimensions of exclusion, to examine the factors that promote processes of exclusion, and to discuss the situation of some excluded groups. Throughout the monograph, the concept of exclusion is related to poverty, unemployment, and the lack of social integration.

# Chapter 1

## Conceptualizing social exclusion in developing countries

### I.   Concepts of social exclusion in Western industrialized countries

The term "social exclusion" is being increasingly used in discussions of the "new poor", "inequality", and "injustice" in Western Europe. Following the lead of the French, social scientists and policy-makers are trying to explain the underlying mechanisms of processes of exclusion to make it possible to find solutions to reverse the process to one of inclusion. Disintegration of social ties between the individual and society is seen as being at the root of social exclusion.

In France, the *Commissariat Général au Plan* limited the definition of social exclusion by considering employment as the core of social ties, social cohesion, and social transactions. Thus, employment is a prerequisite for integration. This approach considers the individual as a production unit in the market economy. Therefore, an individual's inclusion or exclusion is based on his or her participation in the labour force.

The Observatory on National Policies to Combat Social Exclusion, created in 1990 by the Commission of the European Communities, pursued a social rights approach to exclusion. This approach was based on an empirical identification of social exclusion that allows the design and evaluation of practical interventions. Social rights as expressed by "citizenship" was used as the term of reference. This approach looks at the rights of the citizen on a sectorial basis. This addresses questions such as: "What are the social rights of the citizen relating to employment, housing, health care, law, etc...? How effective are national policies in securing these rights?" It also evaluates the ability of citizens to secure their social rights.

Paugum [1993] explains social exclusion as a process of social "disqualification". This is a multi-dimensional process where an individual goes through several stages that lead to exclusion. The first stage is vulnerability due to loss of employment or income. This is followed by a stage of dependence created by difficulties in attaining social services as a result of income insufficiency. The third stage includes a breakdown of social and economic participation due to handicaps such as lack of access to the labour market, housing problems, health problems and family disintegration. Finally, the accumulation of the above problems and the breakdown of social networks results in exclusion.

## II.  The need for different theoretical models of social exclusion in developing countries

The study of social exclusion in developing countries is still in its infancy. Although the general symptoms may appear to be similar to those of industrialized societies, the nature of exclusion in low-income countries should be investigated independently. The new interest in social exclusion comes at a time when an evaluation of the latest experiences of development is badly needed, especially since problems of poverty are increasing and participation in social rights (such as education and employment) seem to be shrinking. Yet the notion of exclusion has already generated considerable controversy among social scientists.[1] On the one hand, some argue that exclusion in a developing country context is no more than another terminology in development discourse that describes poverty. The argument is based on the assumption that poverty and deprivation are synonyms of exclusion. On the other hand, some argue that the difference between the concepts poverty and exclusion is reflected in what each measures. Poverty measures shortfalls in relation to consumption, purchasing power, and social provisioning. Exclusion includes but is not limited to the above measurements. For example, social provisioning, rights to organization, social participation and effective political representation are also viewed within the context of social exclusion. In other words, exclusion is a dynamic process related to social rights, to equal participation in economic and social growth. As Rodgers explains [1994, p. 2]:

---

[1] This is based on discussions of social exclusion which took place at a workshop held by the International Institute for Labour Studies in Cambridge, England, in July 1994.

In none of these areas can it be said the idea of social exclusion offers a fundamentally new approach. But it does offer an alternative way of thinking about social and economic mechanisms underlying inequality... it provides a way of linking together social issues which are normally analysed separately.

At the time this study was conducted, there was no literature on social exclusion in developing countries. Recently, a global project organized by the International Institute for Labour Studies (IILS) and the United Nations Development Programme (UNDP) explored the notion of social exclusion in low-income societies. Silver [1995] attempted to conceptualize a framework for the study of exclusion which could be universally applied. Her analysis consisted of an extensive review of the various definitions and usages of exclusion based on the different conceptions of integration and citizenship in the literature of Western industrialized countries. Silver identified three main "paradigms" of exclusion: the republican, the liberal, and the monopoly. As in most studies conducted in industrialized countries, a common frame of reference for these paradigms of exclusion is the classical sociological theories of solidarity and social integration of Emile Durkheim, Talcott Parson, and Max Weber. The historical experiences of France, Britain, and the United States are used as primary examples.

Exclusion under the "republican paradigm" represents the breaking-up of social ties between the individual and society. This paradigm is strongly influenced by Durkheim. Social order is the individual's acceptance of common values and norms through mediating institutions. Integration is based on "organic solidarity", "collective conscience", and "national consensus". In the "liberal paradigm", exclusion reflects social differentiation and economic specialization. Exclusion may be a result of an individual's choice or may be a consequence of discrimination and market failures. Integration is a voluntary network of exchanges between individuals with independent interests and motivations. Influenced by Parson, this paradigm conceives of integration as a general adherence to common norms and values. Citizenship rights are exercised by the right to choose one's cultural identity and tolerance of differences. In the "monopoly paradigm", exclusion is a consequence of social closures achieved when institutions and cultural distinctions create boundaries and monopolize scarce resources. Society is seen as hierarchical and perpetuates inequalities. This model is influenced by Weber.

Silver believes that these models provide an analytical framework to explore issues of exclusion. They are "ideal types" that may be present in differing mixes in one society. However, as she explains, "choosing one definition means accepting the theoretical and ideological baggage associated with it" [ibid., p. 60].

How useful are Silver's paradigms in explaining processes of exclusion in the context of developing countries such as Yemen? It may be possible to define exclusion at a macro level, i.e. as conceived by the *excluders*, or at the micro level, i.e. as conceived by the *excluded*. At the macro level, the concept of exclusion in Yemen may be understood in the terms of the republican paradigm. Religion has been the primary institution for integration. The state uses Islam as a means of integration and a way to win consensus for its legitimacy. Moral norms are based on Islamic principles. These moral norms represent the "collective conscience". The excluded are those who have failed to establish social ties with society. They have not been able to infiltrate the cultural boundaries of Yemeni society.

At the micro level, social exclusion may be defined within the "monopoly paradigm". Traditional Yemeni social groups represent social closures. Tribal affiliations and other cultural practices, for example, are dynamic factors that influence social identity. As a result, access to land and employment are strongly influenced by social identities and networks based on kinship and friendship between equals. As Gore explains, these social identities regulate access in various ways [1994, p. 22].

Although Silver's paradigms may provide an approach to classifying different processes of social exclusion, it should be noted that the application of these paradigms to the question of social exclusion in developing countries has its pitfalls. These paradigms are a product of studies performed in Western industrialized countries whose social, political and economic experiences are not comparable to those of developing countries. Classical sociological theories of Western Europe and North America may not apply to developing countries. These studies (Durkheim, Parson, Weber, the School of Chicago, and others) looked at the problem of exclusion and integration in relation to social changes in industrial societies. Social order in this context has been transformed by dynamic and destabilizing institutions such as markets, economic individualism and self interest. Social order in industrial societies is no longer based on traditional structural norms [Holton, 1992, p. 189].

Durkheim contrasted the process of integration in traditional societies and in modern societies by contrasting the different social solidarities that hold these societies together and their level of structural differentiation. Social solidarity in traditional societies is based on what he called "mechanical solidarity". In these societies, the strong sense of social identity and cultural practices limit the degree of structural differentiation. This is clearly the case in Yemen. In industrialized countries, social solidarity is based on "organic solidarity" (the basis of Silver's models). This is a process of differentiation that is based on division of labour and individualism. Although they recognize differences, they are still subject to a higher unity [ibid., p. 190].

Weber and Durkheim seem to agree on the importance of social differentiation and value pluralism. Weber's argument is based on rationalization as the predominant integrating force.

Certain explicit cultural practices, such as science and rational law, are major bearers of rationalization. In this sense rationalization does not produce integration simply by spontaneous means without any reference to prevailing structures of meaning. [ibid., p. 199]

Holton argues that the above Occidental characteristics distinguish the West from other civilizations, such as Islam or Confucian China. This does not imply that non-Western civilization do not have dynamic features of their own. As a result of their own history, they did not generate the same type of worldly-rational differentiation of economy and society that the West experienced. Thus, under these conditions, their economies remained strongly embedded in forms of cultural integration that limit the full development of private property rights and market-centred individualism. These conditions limit the social transformation of non-Western cultures in more thoroughly "rationalized" directions.

Yemen has a dual economy rather than a market economy. In other words, some people's livelihood continues to depend on subsistence agriculture and traditional methods of trade. The institutions that mediate moral norms for a "conscious collective" are not the market and the economy. Structural differentiation is not as well developed as in industrialized societies. It continues to be based on cultural identities. Social change has not been strongly influenced by the modest growth of Yemen's economy but rather by political change.

The political dimension is crucial for understanding processes of social exclusion since access to resources and services and entitlement in low-income countries are centred in the distributive powers of the political system. This also includes considering the political stability of the country, which is an important factor essential for understanding social exclusion in developing countries. The *realpolitik* in many developing countries shows that political stability (or instability) is an important determinant of economic development and social change. For example, in countries such as Iraq, Iran, Lebanon, Sudan, Somalia, Jordan and Yemen (in the case of the Gulf War), political crisis brings economic development to a halt. This is frequently initiated by cuts in foreign aid, restrictions on loans from the World Bank and the IMF, and economic embargoes. At the international level, these countries that are excluded from foreign investments lack the credibility to participate in the international market system. At the national level, poverty and deprivations increase and promote processes of exclusion.

Many studies of development overemphasize the role of the market economy and underemphasize that of the political system as a factor that influences economic and social change. Such an approach is clearly influenced by Western models of development. The unpredictabe nature of political systems in many developing States complicates the synthesis of models to explain economic change and social development.

In conclusion, if the political and social systems of developing countries were similar to those of Western societies, Silver's paradigms would have been more useful for explaining the processes of exclusion in developing societies such as Yemen. The Industrial Revolution, the French Revolution, the separation of State and church represent major events that differentiate the historical experiences of the West from those of developing countries. These events have had a profound impact on social relations and economic growth in the West.

Thus, there is a need to develop theoretical models of exclusion that take into account the economic, social, and political factors of "pre-industrial" and "newly industrializing" societies.

## III. The nature of social exclusion in developing countries: Some other views

Other social scientists who have explored the theoretical implications of exclusion have also questioned the appropriateness of using Western models to explain social exclusion in developing countries [Faria, 1995; Gore, 1994, 1995; Wolfe, 1994; Yepez, 1994]. A common theme among these different studies is that, unlike industrialized societies where social exclusion is referred to as the "new poverty", in developing countries it is an old problem. In Western societies the excluded are an outcome of long-term unemployment and poverty. Those vulnerable are those subject to the multiple deprivations of gender, ethnicity and age, as well as immigrants. In developing countries, social exclusion is a structural phenomenon related to poverty, deprivation and inequality. It is closely connected to issues of lack of access to goods and services, and lack of political participation.

Yepez [1994, p. 13] underlines the differences between the notion of social exclusion in developed and developing countries by asking: "Does it make sense to say that those who never benefited from social integration are excluded? Why speak of social exclusion in countries where there has been no welfare state, no pension, no unemployment allocation? Does the notion of social exclusion only refer to the `new poverty' of the West? What does it have in common with the `old poverty' of Latin America?"

Wolfe's study [1994] provides a general framework of issues of exclusion that are of concern to low-income societies. He proposes six dimensions of exclusion that are most prevalent in developing counties. This study is particularly useful since the dimensions of exclusion highlight social and economic trends taking place in developing countries in relation to changes in the global arena. He explains how the different dimensions of exclusion interact with each other and with the efforts toward integration. The six dimensions of exclusion are:

1. *Exclusion from livelihood.* This refers to insecure employment as a consequence of the industrialization process and other destabilizing forces of economic change. This positions individuals to marginal and precarious types of informal labour.

2. *Exclusion from social services, welfare, and security.* Until the 1980s, the right to education, health services, shelter, safe water, sanitation, and other social safety nets were considered the responsibility of the State. Access to these services is now being curtailed as result of governments' inability to maintain the social welfare state and the move towards the privatization of these services.

3. *Exclusion from the consumer culture.* This dimension is concerned with exclusion of people from certain material goods that range from nutrition to electronic goods. Changing norms of consumption often become cultural necessities. Consequently, sentiments of exclusion can be strong among those with income levels that cannot afford these goods.

4. *Exclusion from political choice.* This dimension of exclusion is a result of national and international forces in the global economic order that dictate political decisions with total disregard to popular choice.

5. *Exclusion from bases for popular organization.* This dimension touches on issues of "participation", "organized efforts" and "control".

6. *Exclusion from understanding what is happening.* Information is essential in establishing modern social relations.

Wolfe's study provides an overview of important dimensions of exclusion relevant to developing countries, and thus identifies the nature of social exclusion by addressing the issue of "exclusion from what".

In a review of the Latin America literature, Faria [1995] explains that the term exclusion has not been used with theoretical implications.

However, he points out that the literature on poverty, deprivation and inequality provide useful insight for a conceptual understanding of social exclusion in Latin America. The literature of the 1950s and 1960s provides a broad theoretical basis for conceptualizing structural processes that lead to poverty and deprivation in Latin America as "the mode of social integration" into the world capitalist system. These processes result from the patterns of integration of social groups, families, individuals, and regions into the global division of labour. This approach emphasizes that poverty is not an incidental phenomena, but rather is structurally related to the way economic and social systems function. Faria identifies four processes that sustain poverty and deprivation [ibid., pp. 118-119]. First, poverty and deprivation are related to the rural and agricultural structures prevailing in Latin America and the transformations that are taking place. This includes lack of access to land, to technical assistance, to credits and markets, land tenure patterns, and labour-saving agricultural modernization that has resulted not only in rural/urban migration, but also in urban poverty. Second, poverty is strongly associated with employment trends and the structure of the labour markets such as employment scarcity, lack of protection and instability and vulnerability. Precariousness of employment and the dualization of the urban labour market are seen in relation to the effects of the economic crises of the 1980s, the structural adjustment policies, and the ongoing process of economic restructuring. The third mechanism emphasizes the role of political systems. Fragility of democratic institutions, authoritarianism and lack of political participation are regarded as main determinants of poverty and exclusion. Finally, the fourth mechanism is the lack of adequate education as a principal determinant of poverty and deprivation.

Faria concludes that the concept of social exclusion as defined in the West is context-specific and of limited relevance to the notion of exclusion in Latin America [ibid., p. 127]. It conveys ideas that reflect situations where international immigrants form a strong component of the poor and where there are major ethnic, religious and cultural differences in the population. This is not applicable to societies which are both politically and culturally homogeneous, such as those of Latin America. Faria therefore suggests that the formulation of the concept of social exclusion should be viewed in a more general framework that provides ways of integrating loosely connected notions such as poverty, deprivation and lack of access to goods, services and assets, and precariousness of social rights. More specifically, he proposes the examination of social exclusion by addressing the issue of "exclusion by what", since this approach is more appropriate to the Latin America context.

Gore [1994, 1995] examined the notion of social exclusion in Africa. Based on his review of the African literature, he concluded that social exclusion in Africa cannot be defined as an outcome of processes of poverty and unemployment whereby an individual loses membership in society [1995, pp. 104-105]. Rather, the nature of exclusion should be considered within the broader context of social membership from participation in public life. In other words, group memberships and social identities such as ethnicity, religion, and gender affect entitlement to a range of resources and social goods. In industrialized countries, the process of exclusion is based on the legal relationship between the citizen and the state. The most important of the social rights of the citizen is the right to employment. In contrast, exclusion in Africa is based on the relationship defined in membership of, and status within, groups and networks of various kinds [1995, pp. 103-105]. Social rights are not yet fully nationalized but are also based on customary laws. Factors such as colonialization, customary laws, rights of nationalization, and land tenure practices explain the social order and structures of social exclusion [1994, p. 16]. The trajectories of exclusion must also be understood in relation to the history of African societies, the strategies and practices of Africans themselves, and the logic of their actions and not in terms of correspondence and deviations from ideal Western models.[2]

Gore points out that the African literature yields to the formulation of a concept of exclusion, which is not "Eurocentric" and can be treated as an analytical concept to explain the process of exclusion rather than just a descriptive outcome of the process. Thus, social exclusion as an analytical concept is based on the following four processes [1995, pp. 106-111]. The first is the nationality of social exclusion. In this approach, the identity of social exclusion is defined in relation to the state and the institutionalization of exclusionary practices. In the case of Africa, the rights of access to goods and services and other associated obligations have not been fully nationalized. The second is the relationship between social identity and rules of entitlement. Access to resources and social goods depends on membership of groups and networks, and social identity is an important element in the rules of membership. The third is the relationship between exclusionary and inclusionary practices. This analyses exclusionary practices within the broader context in which people are integrated into an economy and society. This is predominantly based on the analyses of clientalist networks and where patrons compete for clients in a struggle for

---

[2] Yepez also points out that there are differences in the analyses of social exclusion in neighbouring countries such as France and Belgium [Yepez, 1994, p. 12].

key resources and services. These relationships are not static but change over time. The final approach is the analysis of social exclusion and the economic crises. This takes into account how these relationships are affected by economic change.

Hence, Gore addresses the issue of "exclusion by whom". An important contribution of Gore's study is its emphasis on the role of social identities and social order in processes of exclusion. Social relationships are based on these factors which play a central role in processes of inclusion and exclusion in primordial societies. As mentioned earlier, less industrialized countries do not have the high degree of structural differentiation of Western society. Social solidarity continues to be established on cultural practices. Therefore, analysis of social order is crucial for understanding processes of social exclusion in developing countries.

Faria, Gore, and Wolfe highlight the multidimensional structure of social exclusion. A common frame of reference for Latin America and Africa is the fact that social exclusion is closely connected to structural poverty and deprivation. However, Faria and Gore differ in the identi-fication of the processes of exclusion. As a result, those subjected to exclusion differ. In Africa, the excluded are those who are not capable of attaining social membership at the group level. In Latin America, the excluded are identified as those not integrated into the social division of labour. These differences between both studies are significant and clearly illustrate how processes of social exclusion are country-specific.[3] Nonetheless, the differences that emerge from conceptualizing social exclusion in various regions of the world are important since they allow for traits to be recognized; hence they provide in-depth insight to what is involved in the study of social exclusion in developing countries.

## IV. The concept of social exclusion in Yemen

The studies described above raise two important issues that should be considered in conceptualizing social exclusion in Yemen. First, the problem of processes of exclusion is identified as it relates to the society under study. This provides the boundaries of the definition of exclusion. As is the case in the countries of sub-Saharan Africa [Gore, 1995] and Latin America [Faria, 1995], exclusion in Yemen is associated with lack of access to goods

---

[3] Yepez [1994] points out that there are differences in the analyses of social exclusion even between neighbouring countries such as Belgium and France.

and services, and lack of participation. However, the process of social exclusion in Yemen can only be partially explained by social identity (as is the case in Africa) or the economic system (as is the case in Latin America). Second, the contextual setting of exclusion is highlighted. The processes of exclusion in both regions (sub-Saharan Africa and Latin America) are consistent with transitional societies and with governments that are not highly institutionalized. The former explains structural social attributes such as cultural norms passed from one generation to the next such as social identity. The latter explains the limitation of state interventions in promoting economic and social development. Both factors overlap and contribute to processes of exclusion.

Developing countries are often characterized as dual societies. This dualism reflects a state of transition in which traditional beliefs and practices endure, and conflict with efforts to transform society into a modern state. Hence, dualism is reflected in the economic, political, and social systems. Dualism is fundamental for understanding social change and economic development in Yemen and is also instrumental in explaining social exclusion.

The social culture in traditional societies is based on close personal relationships at the level of the family, the tribe, and the communal group. This is also the base from which values are derived, unlike those of the State which are regarded as more abstract. These structural norms bind society. In other words, they represent mechanisms of inclusion within the social order. The gradual change in structures of these societies results in shifts in the distribution of wealth and the realignment of individuals and groups supporting or opposing various economic policies. As Huntington explains [1965], in the political realm, changing social and economic conditions affect the bases of political power and the groups that compete for positions of influence and authority. The authority of conservative traditional leaders is challenged by those who have achieved popular acclaim for their radical programmes and by those who have attained control over new instruments of power. These usually consist of modern military forces, bureaucracies, and economic institutions. Differences in the duration of time of transition and in the problems encountered by these societies during this period reflect the variety of traditional bases from which they have evolved. A political system that is characterized by low-level institutionalization and by a lack of functionally specific institutions (such as separate religious, tribal, and political authorities and institutions) is another major characteristic of transitional societies. In such countries, the state considers social integration to be a national goal since it is a means for establishing its authority, unifying society, and proceeding towards development. Primarily, this is translated into national policy by social and economic development. These national development policies represent "modern" mechanisms of inclusion which are targeted to displace the traditional mechanisms. As a result, social membership is transformed from one that is based on personal relationships and the communal group to one that is based on citizenship and membership in the broader national community. This has been the case in Yemen.

Social exclusion in transitional societies is also dualistic in nature. On the one hand, individuals or groups most vulnerable to exclusion are those that are external to the social order, or the traditional legal code. Their exclusion from social membership is passive and discriminatory. Although the rights of the excluded may be nationally protected, their exclusion is enforced by the way people behave. As is the case in most traditional practices, this social behaviour is resistant to change. On the other hand, social exclusion in the more modern state may be embedded in national development policies. Such exclusion may arise from the lack of access of citizens to resources and services. Processes of exclusion are put into motion as a result of the unequal distribution of development benefits. Thus, the state's efforts to integrate society and transform it into a modern state by means of social and economic development (such as provision of education and training, health services, public roads, water and sanitation, and other basic services), citizens with no access to such services are excluded from their social rights and thus from the development process. This deprivation results in poverty and marginal participation in society. The inability of the state to reach all segments of society through its development efforts is often due to its limitations of skilled human power, physical infrastructure, inappropriate development planning, and financial constraints. Furthermore, despite the low level of institutionalization in most cases of these countries, they remain highly centralized. They are frequently unwilling to share the responsibility of decision-making in development planning and policies with regional representatives. Consequently, development projects are mired in a labyrinth of bureaucracy and are frequently ineffective for meeting the need and the demands of society. These deficiencies are often perceived by the excluded as evidence of the inefficiency of the government and its inability to protect rightful access to all the benefits of development. Such perceptions intensify traditional social ties and distance the State from society. In some cases, the problem is compounded by the lack of effective official representatives who can objectively represent the interests of the weaker constituents. This creates another dimension of exclusion, i.e. exclusion from representation. Rights to effective political representation is often a sensitive issue in developing countries since it raises questions of democracy, equality, and participation.

Social exclusion resulting from the social order or national development policies are not mutually exclusive; the two can interact in dual societies. For example, this may be observed in political systems in which the powerful traditional elites — such as tribal leaders — establish close links with the modern political system and manage to manoeuvre the limited goods and services to their segments of society. "Exclusion is not something that just happens. It is a practice of the more powerful" [Gore, 1995, p. 113]. Hence, inclusion in development benefits such as education and employment opportunities are available to those who have access to either one or both of the inclusionary mechanisms in dual societies.

## V.  Conclusion

Social exclusion is best understood as a process in relation to social membership in a particular society. Social relations and networks maintain this process of membership, and assert integration into the mainstream of society. That is, social relations establish networks, and networks regulate access to social services, employment, and social and political participation.

Social exclusion is not a new phenomenon. It is an old and universal social problem. In every society, there are individuals and/or groups which are not accepted or have problems integrating in their communities. What is new in the evolving concept of social exclusion is the notion of exclusion as it relates to modern economic changes and social ties.

In Western Europe unemployment, poverty, dependency, vulnerability, and marginalization are regarded as symptoms of the exclusion process. These symptoms are reflected in the increasing numbers of the homeless, the deterioration of the urban slums, the long-term unemployed, and the precarious situations of immigrants and ethnic minorities. Social exclusion, however, is not limited to deprivation from the means to improve one's livelihood. Rather, it is a broader conception of disadvantage which relates both to a citizen's rights to a livelihood as well as to social and political rights.

In transitional dual societies, social membership can be based on either the traditional social order or the modern economy state. In primordial societies, the social contract is based on kinship and a traditional legal code that ensures for its members the rights to livelihood. However, at the national level, the notion of citizenship and their rights to social, economic and political participation is still in a state of flux in transitional developing countries. Both have prerequisites for inclusion and thus foster processes of social exclusion. This is an essential approach in understanding social exclusion in Yemen.

It is also an approach that could be relevant to some countries more than others, and particularly relevant to dual (transitional) societies. Suffice it to say, the diverse interpretations of social exclusion in different regions of the world reflect the complexity of formulating a theoretical model for a notion which is strongly embedded in the way societies function culturally.

# Chapter 2

## The rise of dualism: Changing bases of social integration and processes of social exclusion at the macro level

All existing things have a past. Nothing which happens escapes completely from the grip of the past; some events scarcely escape at all from its grip... Entities, events, or systems, physiological, psychological, social and cultural, have careers in which at one point the state of the system stands in some determinate relationship to the state at earlier points. [Shils]

It is essential to define the nature of social integration in a country in order to understand processes of exclusion. Once the structures that hold the social fabric are identified, one can then proceed to analyse the processes of exclusion. This chapter examines three significant periods of Yemen's experience of political change — before and after unification — and the ideologies of national integration associated with them. The objective is to explain the transition of society into a state of dualism with dual processes of exclusion. The focus is on social change in relation to political change and economic and social development, and the way in which the interaction of these factors affects processes of social exclusion.

The chapter makes it apparent that social integration has always been considered a major challenge to government and a pertinent socio-political and economic issue throughout Yemen's political history. The government has recognized that social and economic development is critical to alleviate poverty, unite society, and establish government authority. As a result, this would advance the development and transformation of society into a modern economy state. An underlying goal has been to transfer social memberships from those based on traditional structural norms to one based on civil rights and the national community, consequently undermining the autonomy of sub-groups.

The heterogeneity of Yemeni society is observed in tribal allegiances, political affiliations, religious sects, and geographic dispersion. These sub-groups in society represent social closures where in most cases social membership is primarily a birthright. The deep-rooted structural divisions in society have been a hindrance to the transition of society into a modern state.

# I. The primordial society: The pre-transformation period

The strategic location of Yemen between the Red Sea and the Indian Ocean led to fierce competition between the Ottomans and the British for a foothold in the country in the late nineteenth century. This was settled in 1914 with an agreement that led to the division of Yemen into two separate states — North and South Yemen. Following this division, social and economic development in the North and South took different routes that were largely influenced by their different political experiences.

The Hamid-al-Din Imams' era in North Yemen (1918-1962), and British occupation in South Yemen (1897-1967), illustrate the primordial Yemeni society and its structures of social integration and exclusion.

## 1. The Mutawaklite Kingdom of Yemen

In North Yemen, Ottoman presence was limited to the Tihama coast. The highlands remained independent, consisting primarily of tribal confederations that were governed by the principles of an Islamic state, i.e. an Imamate. In this case, the political leader and the religious leader — the Imam — were one and the same. The Imam was granted absolute authority in spiritual and civil matters. This Yemeni state had been an independent Islamic state since the seventh century and was one of the very few countries in the world that was never colonized.

In 1919, Imam Yahya Hamid-al-Din successfully overthrew the Ottomans. He then set out to unite the country under his rule. Primarily, this consisted of integrating the highland tribes and the lowland settlers who had been under direct Ottoman rule. (Several unsuccessful attempts were also made to liberate the South from the British.) The new Imamate was known as the Mutawaklite Kingdom of Yemen, the term *Mutawakalite* meaning "under the guidance of Allah". The Imamate considered itself a sacred collective system, functioning on the idea that whatever is good for the community is good for the individual [Zabarah, 1983, p. 2]. It abided by higher laws than those of kinship or clan, and these higher laws were the basis for its continuity. The state was governed by the Islamic legal code the *Sharia'a* according to the Zaydi doctrine.[4] According to Zaydi jurisprudence, Imam Yahya, who was a *sayyid*, was considered the legitimate ruler of the country.

Islam was considered to provide the moral norms to integrate and establish solidarity among the different groups in the country. What helped enhance the Imam's effort of social integration under his regime was that Yemeni belief that the Imam was blessed and possessed spiritual powers derived from his direct descent from the Prophet. His status was reinforced by his successful military campaigns against the Ottomans and his ability to unite the whole northern parts of the country. Thus, the idea of a country unified under the banner of Islam was strongly welcomed by society.

In his efforts to maintain Yemen as a strict Islamic state, Imam Yahya totally isolated Yemen from the rest of the world. His policies prohibited both Yemenis and foreigners from entering and leaving the country without his permission. Secular education was banned and interaction with foreign states was limited [Zabarah, 1982, p. 160]. This "isolationist" policy had a very significant effect on the country as a whole and on the Yemeni people as individuals. As the rest of the world was experiencing major economic, social, and political changes, the Yemeni people were left behind.

## A. Restricted social and economic development

Imam Yahya's policies restricted social development and economic activities with the outside world. This led to economic stagnation, widespread poverty, and feelings of social backwardness. The Imam justified his actions as an effort to protect the country from foreign invasion and exploitation, a phenomena most neighbouring countries in the region were undergoing. He also presented it as a means to preserve the country's national and religious identity.

Despite these justifications, there was a growing feeling among society that they were excluded from progress and modernization. Not only were

---

[4] Fifty-five per cent of the population, predominantly those in the highlands, are Zaydi-Shia; and 45 per cent, predominantly in the lowlands, are Shafii-Sunni. The Zaydi sect of Islam broke away from the Shia sect because of disagreement concerning the succession of the next caliphate. The Zaydi principal belief holds that, although the Imam must be a descendant of the Prophet, i.e. a *sayyid*, he is elected according to his merits and not just by the familial inheritance rule. Another characteristic that distinguishes the Zaydi sect from the remaining Shia sect is their insistence that the Imam is immanent rather than in a hidden phase.

basic services such as water and electricity non-existent, but health and education services were minimal. For example, Imam Yahya used education as a major tool for preserving religious ideology. This was incorporated into the educational system by undermining secular education and emphasizing religious schooling. The Imam feared that subversive foreign ideas could be infiltrated through schooling. Thus, the primary curriculum was restricted to reading, writing, arithmetic, and learning the Quran. The country's limited resources were reflected in the restricted educational system. There were few boys' schools, most of them in the major cities. Girls' education was not socially acceptable at the time. As a result, education was more accessible to boys in the cities. More access to education was made possible through private tutors, most of whom were religious scholars [Hashem, 1992, pp. 10-11]. However, this was also primarily accessible to children of affluent families. Only relatively few children in rural areas went to the mosques to be taught how to read and write. Other public services were also limited during this period. For example, there was a single postal service with one post officer for all Sana'a, two telephone lines — one from Sana'a to Hodeidah, the other from Sana'a to Taiz; and a telegraph network left behind by the Turks. The major source of income of the state came from two sources: *zakat* and Customs. The *zakat* is the Islamic tax assessed on agriculture, livestock, production, and wealth. Traditionally, it was collected by the *shaykhs* of the village. The taxes were considered high by the taxpayers, whose property had occasionally suffered natural disasters such as floods or droughts. Customs came primarily from the caravans passing through Yemen and the port of Hodiedah.

The country as a whole became impoverished as a consequence of the scarcity of available resources. People's livelihoods were affected since the limited infrastructure and economic stagnation deprived individuals from any employment opportunities. This restricted a large number of *Zaydis* in the highlands to farming under impoverished conditions. The *Shafiis*, who were more or less in control of foreign trade because of their location along the coastal regions, were also constrained.[5] Imam Yahya did not trust foreign trade to remain in their hands and thus took direct measures to restrict their economic influence. This was implemented by increasing the taxes and Customs and appointing inexperienced agents, chosen by the

---

[5] *Shafiis* belong to one of the four schools of Sunni Islam, which recognizes that the right to the caliphate is by election and not by inheritance. Although the *Shafiis* did not recognize the Imam's "religious" right to head the State, during the Hamid al-Din regime they acknowledged the Imam's position as temporal head of state.

Imam, to take over control of foreign trade [Stookey, 1974, p. 201].[6] Many rich *Shafii* merchants conducted most of their trade from Aden and kept their money there as well. Smaller *Shafii* merchants often emigrated to Aden for extended periods of time to earn their living, while others emigrated abroad and established themselves in places such as Cardiff (Wales); Marseilles (France); and Djibouti (Africa).

## B.   The social order and social exclusion

Imam Yahya relied on a rigid hierarchy of elites in administering the country. Primarily, Imam Yahya's sons came directly under him in terms of political importance.[7] They were followed by the *sayyids* and the *qadis*. The Imam was reluctant, however, to delegate too much authority to the *sayyids* since he was cautious of the fact that in *Zaydi* doctrine any *sayyid* who had the qualifications of an Imam could take over the rule. Finally, there were the *shaykhs*, whom the Imam depended on for their tribal military power. The two most powerful tribal confederations were *Bakil* and *Hashid*. There was a great dependency on personalities in the political system, since there were no effective formal institutions. Authority was delegated according to who was trusted by the Imam at the time.

The principal structural norm that defined social membership in the social order was genealogy. This social order also represented closures of sub-groups, and played an important role in determining access to social and economic participation. The less traceable one's genealogy, the lower the social status one had in society. Furthermore, social status correlated with occupation. As one's position in the social order descended so did economic activity, while the barriers encountered in social and economic participation increased. For example, people who lived in towns and villages and worked as small merchants and artisans were considered *du'afa* (weak). These groups, of less traceable descent, had no common descent group to support them, nor did they control any land. Those at the very end of the social order were those whose genealogy was not traceable or unknown. Consequently, they were confined to the lowest means of economic activity. This group was represented by the *akhdam*.

---

[6] Although the Imam curtailed the activities of the merchants, none of his officials had the expertise, for example, to arrange the overhaul of the Imam's aircraft, or to order supplies for the government hospitals. For such services, the Imam relied completely on one *Shafii* merchant, Shaykh Mohammad Al-Jabalie, who was considered to also have monopolized Yemen's foreign trade [Al-Attar, 1965, p. 306].

[7] Imam Yahya had 14 sons who were given the title of *Sayf al-Islam* (the swords of Islam) meaning the warriors and protectors of Islam.

In 1948, Imam Yahya was assassinated. His son, Prince Ahmad, inherited the Imamate. Imam Ahmad did not completely abolish the "isolationist policy" but modified it due to crucial political and economic needs which his government alone could not fulfill. This change was primarily implemented in foreign policy. Imam Ahmad joined the Confederation of the United Arab Republic. He also sent a group of military cadets for training in Egypt and Iraq, and allowed students to study abroad. Even within this confined exposure to the outside world, foreign ideas infiltrated into the country. This made Yemenis more aware of their economic and social deprivations, since they were able to compare their situation with what was taking place in the outside world.

On 18 September 1962, Imam Ahmad, who had survived a couple of attempts at assassination and coups, died from natural causes, and his son Al-Badr succeeded him as Imam. The act of appointing an Imam by inheritance was a violation of the *Zaydi* jurisprudence, since the Imamate was by election and not inheritance. This was another source of resentment towards of the Hamid-al-Din Imams and their loss of legitimacy. Imam Al-Badr ruled Yemen for eight days. Although he had initiated his governing by promising political reform and economic and social development, he was overthrown by a *coup d'état*, which brought an end to the Hamid-al-Din reign and the primordial state of the Imamate.

## 2.    The Federation of South Arabia

In contrast to the experience of the North, the British colonizers in the South were not interested in promoting social integration. Rather, their political objectives consisted of maintaining a weak and fragmented society. The British began their occupation in Aden and gradually extended north and eastward to include what came to be known as the Western and Eastern Protectorates. Aden was made part of the British Indies. In 1937, it became a separate Crown Colony. The British were primarily interested in turning Aden into a major port in order to control the trade routes along the Indian Ocean.

In the hinterlands in the South, the British presence was rudimentary. The emphasis was on exerting indirect control within the framework of the status quo, and minimizing the costs and potential risks of involvement by refraining from encouraging social and economic development.

The political status of the hinterlands consisted of a complex set of sultanates of various sizes and powers that represented mini states. There was no sense of nationhood among these statelets. Each statelet consisted of several tribal areas ruled by a common sultan, who was a member of the *sayyid*class. The tribes were intensely fragmented; unlike their counterparts in the North, they had no strong confederations. Traditionally, several tribal groups came together to select the sultan. The sultan then acted as head of state, contingent on tribal support. The British eventually granted various sultans and notables formal status under their watchful eye. This was implemented by adding a single colonial authority at the head to police relationships among its constituent elements. Ismael & Ismael [1986, pp. 9-10] explain that, in so doing, the British caused the social structure to become more rigid. Before colonial intrusion, sultans and *shaykhs* had been relatively accountable for their actions. It was not uncommon for incompetent or brutal leaders to be removed by those by whom they were selected. The balance of power changed constantly as each group vied for a better position and greater power vis-à-vis its neighbours. The British changed this structure of relationships. Under the protectorate treaty system, a sultan's position and the existing intra- and inter-tribal status quo were guaranteed by the overwhelming power of the British, reducing a sultan's reliance on those under him. At the same time, the British instigated suspicion and hostility among the various sultans and *shaykhs* in order to diffuse any possible alliances, and maintain the ultimate authority of the British. As the sultans of South Yemen grew more powerful and less accountable, they also became regarded as collaborators with the foreign colonizers. Economic disparity widened between tribal confederations that were relatively wealthy and poor agricultural populations sparsely settled over an immense area of land and governed indirectly through subsidies and along traditional lines [Stookey, 1982, p. 3]. Discontent in the hinterlands with the status quo was channelled into anti-colonialism, which also included the traditional elite.

## Processes of exclusion

Social exclusions were prevalent in both urban and rural areas, based on social identity. Aden, had a rigid social hierarchy based on ethnicity. The Europeans were at the head of the hierarchy followed by, in descending order, the East Indian merchants and civil servants, Arab artisans and workers, the unskilled Yemeni and Somali labourers, and finally the *akhdam*. Most of the urban workers who were of low socio-economic status in Aden under the British hierarchy were from the tribal class and had migrated to Aden in search of work. Lackner [1985, p. 108] points out that the contradiction in the tribes' dual class status influenced their political anti-colonial sentiments and position during the struggle for independence. This social hierarchy also defined social relationships. Neighourhoods, for example, were segregated by ethnic identity and economic status [Ismael & Ismael, 1986, p. 8].

In the hinterlands, similar to the situation in North Yemen, the traditional social order was based on genealogy, which regulated social and economic inclusions and exclusions. At the head of this hierarchy were the *sayyids*, followed by the tribes, the peasants, and finally the *akhdam*. The sultans and *shaykhs* in the countryside owned the majority of land, and controlled grazing rights, water rights, and land allocation. Eighty per cent of the land was cultivated by tenant farmers, agriculture labourers were exploited, and periodic famines were commonplace. Similarly, patterns of subsistence and semi-feudal production existed in the coastal fishing sector, where 13,000 private fisherman were dominated by the fish merchants and local chiefs who owned most of the nets, the larger boats, and other means of production [ibid., p. 80]. The British also played a part in promoting social exclusions. For example, they encouraged the traditional elites' exploitative methods. The British also excluded rural people from social development. Unlike in Aden, the British did not provide rural people with development projects such as schools and hospitals, or the construction of roads that would link the country together. As a result, the country underwent a process of bifurcation — a modernized Aden and a stagnating countryside. This was also accompanied by cultural, economic, and social transformations. For example, in Aden, the colonial social policies used education as a tool to infiltrate Western political idealogy. Different missionary schools were established. The education of girls as well as boys was emphasized.

Hence, South Yemen under British colonialism represented social exclusions that are overt in nature. An absence of strong mediating norms to bind society meant that it was more intensely fragmented. Although the social order was similar to that of the North, Islam was not employed to unite society, since this was not within the political objectives of the British. The social order, however, did define social membership and access to resources and services. Gradually, however, the consequences of exploitation and strong deprivation on people's livelihoods were a unifying force that integrated people and set the stage for a new political system that was to adopt a radical approach for social integration and social and economic development.

## II. The transformation process:
## The Yemen Arab Republic
## and the People's Democratic Republic of Yemen

During the transformation period, society is introduced to a process of social change in which intervening forces attempt to replace the traditional social structures based on personal relationships and group solidarities with norms based on division of labour and meritocracy. Structural differentiation, therefore, is transformed from one contingent on "mechanical solidarity" to one contingent on "organic solidarity".

North Yemen's Revolution of 1962 and South Yemen's Independence in 1967 were major turning points that signified the initiation of the transformation process. Both Yemens rid themselves of their oppressive regimes, and this provided them with a green light for their transformation into modern economy states. Each country adopted a different economic ideology. The North aimed for a free-market-oriented state, while the South aimed for a national socialist state. The new leaders were desperately searching for a new and viable formula around which they could build a consensus that would mobilize and integrate society, and thus legitimize their authority.

Social and economic development was considered the primary means for national integration. Social services such as education, training, and health care were declared available free of charge in both countries. As in many revolutionary governments, social welfare symbolized citizens' rights to equality of participation. However, both states were confronted with a society suffering from severe poverty, a great demand for basic services, unemployment, limited resources, lack of skilled manpower, and limited infrastructure. Thus, transformation was more complex than the revolutionists had calculated. What followed was a period of political instability and economic confusion, which affected the distribution of goods and services and gave rise to new processes of social exclusion.

### 1. Transformation by accommodation:
### The Yemen Arab Republic

On 26 September 1962, a group of military cadets overthrew the Imamate regime in North Yemen and established what became known as the Yemen Arab Republic (YAR). The Imam's opponents declared that their revolution was not directed against Islam, but was a revolt against the Hamid-al-Din Imams' violations of Islam, which calls for progress and modernization. Hence, the new leaders attempted to legitimize their claims by backing them with the *Sharia'a*, and promises of equitable social and economic development.

The revolutionaries announced that all Yemenis are equal citizens before the law [Al-Attar, 1965, p. 304], the State was to be secular, and Islam was the main religion of the country. Fundamentally, this aimed to abolish the traditional political and social base of the Imamate regime, and thus to eliminate the privileges and power given to the *sayyids*, *qadis*, and *shaykhs* — the upper echelon of the social order. As a result, participation was to be based on merit and no longer on an individual's descendence in the social order.

The 1962 Revolution reflected political divisions that included traditional groups and the emergence of "modern" groups. Each group had its own interpretation of the meaning of social and economic progress. The new regime of republicans primarily consisted of the military and the intelligentsia who aimed for revolutionary change. Members of these groups had lived outside the country and had witnessed the political changes taking place in the Middle East, such as the permeating idealogy of nationalism and Pan Arabism.[8] They hoped to achieve change by transforming the traditional social and political systems to a modern economy state. To them these objectives represented an end to structural poverty and inequality. Traditional elites such as the *sayyids* and *qadis*, on the other hand, wanted change by means of reform. This group sought to preserve the Imamate rule, yet under a constitutional monarchy.[9] Such royalists also believed that social and economic reform should be implemented, but in adherence to the principles of Islam. As for the two most powerful tribes — *Bakil* and *Hashid* — the former supported the royalists while the latter supported the republicans. Along with these political divisions were religious divisions. The majority of *Shafiis* supported the republicans, since they sought to end the theocratic regime, which had situated them at the lower end of the social oligarchy. They believed that they had little chance of upward mobility as long as the traditional structures of power were maintained. The two opposing camps — royalists and republicans — had strong financial and military backing from foreign countries, particularly Saudi Arabia, which

---

[8] For example, the group of military officers that led the revolution had been sent by Imam Ahmad for military training in Iraq and Egypt, and there they also received political indoctrination. The intelligentsia was composed of members of the Ahrar party, who had defected to Cairo after the failure of the 1948 coup to overthrow the Imam. The prominent leaders of this movement were Ahmad Muhamad Nu'man and Mohammad Al-Zubayri.

[9] The *sayyids'* group were also considered as the "liberals". This movement was led by Ibrahim Al-Wazir, called "The Society for Yemeni Struggle". The *qadis* were primarily interested in electing an Imam according to the *Zaydi* doctrine.

backed the royalists, and Egypt, which backed the republicans. As a result of these strong political divisions and the inability of the military regime to gain legitimacy, civil war broke out.

The war ended in 1967 with the republicans confirming their leadership of the country. Between the years 1967 and 1992, the YAR had four presidents (Abdul Rahman Al-Iryani, 1967-1974); Ibrahim Al-Hamdi, 1974-1977; Mohammad Al-Gashmi, 1977-1978; and Ali Abdullah Saleh, 1978-1992). Each president came to power as a result of political conflict. Presidents Al-Hamdi and Al-Gashmi were assassinated. Al-Gashmi served for a very short period of time. President Saleh was the last president of the YAR and the first president of the Republic of Yemen. Each left his own personal imprint of social integration and social and economic development.[10] However, this section primarily focuses on Al-Iryani's administration, since it laid the foundation for the transformation of society to a "modern state" and dualism.

The initiation of the transformation process and the establishment of a modern state was to give rise to fundamental questions concerning the mediating norms that were to replace the traditional norms to unite society and legitimize the authority of the leadership. The principal question was the role Islam would have in the new political and social order. Already, preceding the revolution, the first attempt of the military regime to undermine the role of Islam by declaring the country a secular State had led to the loss of support of many allies, and then to the loss of the regime's legitimacy. Al-Attar explains that the military regime's declaration of a "secular" State pushed many tribes into the royalist camp during the war [Al-Attar, 1965, p. 305]. The Imams had promoted Islam as the source of the mediating norms to unite society and establish their authority. In principle, problems of poverty and exclusions were not blamed on Islam but on the political leadership. This was demonstrated by society's desire to maintain Islamic principles as the overall norms of society during the civil war. The complexity of this matter, however, comes from the inability to separate religious norms from traditional structural norms that are inter-related in defining the social order in Yemen.

President Al-Iryani, the first President after the end of the civil war, came from the qadi class. He initiated his leadership by proclaiming the Constitution on the principles of Islam. More specifically, the *Sharia'a* according to *Zaydi* jurisprudence was to continue to direct the governing of the State. These principles were to be the cornerstone for national integration and social and economic development.

---

[10] With the exception of Al-Gashmi whose presidency lasted for only six months.

We shall have no life to live among nations and we can claim no pride or character except through our true Islamic religion which has been the religion of our nation through the last fourteen centuries, and through following the divine guidance achieving its precepts, abiding by its directions and strictures, and by remaining within its bounds. Our Islamic religion, with its directions; magnanimity and breadth is synonymous with development, marches with time, and does not stand as an obstacle in the path of progress in life.[11] (The Permanent Constitution of the YAR, 1971)

## A. The institutionalization of the YAR and strategies of accommodation

The duration and direction of the transformation process depends on the dynamics of the state institutions. The Government considered the creation of its infrastructure essential for the transformation of the state from a traditional to a modern economy state. These institutions were to be the State's machinery for implementing its policies and the delivery of goods and services to the people.

The following strategies were taken in the establishment of the infrastructure of the YAR government institutions. First, Egypt, which had assisted the revolutionaries during the war, was also asked to assist in building the government's infrastructure. The Egyptian experts had no knowledge of the Yemeni environment and needs such as the available manpower, skills, capital and other resources necessary for the establishment of these institutions. These experts merely duplicated the Egyptian organizational structures and by-laws [Al-Abiadah, 1983, p. 2]. Second, due to the lack of skilled personnel to work in these institutions, the government re-employed people who had worked in government positions prior to the revolution. Al-Abiadah explains that many of them brought with them their traditional values and concepts which created various kinds of resistance, directly and indirectly, to the modernization of the administration. Furthermore, as a result of the Treaty of Jeddah, 1970, the government incorporated prominent royalist politicians in the new government.[12] This was intended to symbolize a peace initiative that would bring an end to the civil war and to integrate the different factions under the new state. Third, tribal *shaykhs* from the *Zaydi* northern sections of the country, who had been sympathetic to the republicans during the civil war, were incorporated into the new regime. Lacking the resources to have direct rule over the

---

[11] Translated by A.I. Dawisha, "Document the Permanent Constitution of the YAR", *Middle East Journal*, No. 25 (Summer 1971), p. 389.

[12] These politicians were *sayyids* but not from the Hamid al-Din family.

entire country, the Government gave way to village *shaykhs* to maintain security and order in their villages. Thus, the legitimacy of the *shaykhs'* power was transferred from the traditional state of the Imamate into the "modern" state of the Republic.[13] The tribal *shaykhs'* political participation was further enhanced when they were promoted into prestigious official positions in the central Government, which they continue to hold up to the present. Tribes were also recruited into the army and police. Finally, the *qadis*, who were considered the most qualified to adjudicate litigation and perform administrative functions according to the *Zaydi* system of rule and jurisprudence, were given senior government positions [Stookey, 1974, p. 251]. By implication, this asserted the legitimacy of Al-Iryani's regime by the fact that those who made decisions for the state were eminently qualified in Islamic jurisprudence.

President Al-Iryani perceived his policies as concomitant with the goals of the 1962 Revolution. However, his accommodation strategies undermined the transformation of the country into a modern state and gave rise to dualism. The social order and political order, similar to that of the Imamate regime, continued to be inter-related under the republican regime.This is with the exception of the *sayyids*. Altough some *sayyids* were recruited into government for political objectives, the *sayyids* were stripped of their privileges.[14] In addition, no land reform was implemented other than the nationalization of the Hamid-al-Din's property, sustaining the status quo of land ownership. The establishment of the government institutions indicates how traditional social structures were institutionalized alongside modern structures in the formation of the modern state. Thus, the new Republic state did not really break down the structures of the traditional social order and the privileges that accompanied them. Social membership and networks continued to determine access to resources and services, and participation in them, consequently transforming structural norms of inclusions and exclusions into the modern state.

## B.   Social integration by social and economic development

Social integration during this period can be observed at two different levels. First, at the political level, it was carried out by integrating opposing factions into the political system. Second, at a social level, the process of

---

[13] Tribal *shaykhs* were never given official government positions during the Imamate regime.

[14] Many Yemenis from the other classes of the social order continue to maintain feelings of resentment towards the *sayyids* in the country.

integration was to be followed up by means of social and economic development. Policies such as education, public health, the infrastructure (construction of roads, water systems, etc.) were all intended to provide different services to the people and to represent government efforts at change and development. People's expectations of their government was high as a result of these promises.

Development efforts were initiated by the creation of the Central Planning Organization (CPO) in 1972 and the Three Year Development Plan (1973/74-1975/76). This plan laid down the foundation of the country's infrastructure. However, development projects were constantly interrupted during this period. This was primarily due to the tensions among polarized factions in government. The accommodation of traditionalist and modernist groups in government proved to be fragile when it came to decision-making regarding the direction and pace of development and the transformation of society. The traditionalists consisted mainly of two groups: (1) conservative groups, primarily from the intelligentsia, who wanted to ensure that social and economic development policies did not impinge on the norms of Islam; and (2) tribal *shaykhs* whose influence in government had strengthened, but also felt threatened that the transformation of society into a modern economy would lead to a shift of the allegiance of their tribes from them towards the central government [Hashem, 1984, p. 163-165]. The modernists, who mainly came from among the technocrats and the military, were eager to expedite social and economic development and the transformation of the country. Although the modernists did not have the military strength as the *shaykhs*, they were nonetheless of great importance to the state because they were the only group capable of assisting the government in building the economic and social infrastructure of the country. Different political personalities from both factions were known for their political stance; thus, it was always obvious who had the upper hand simply by the personalities who occupied the important positions in government. Furthermore, the different political factions had external financial backing which influenced ongoing political instability and economic slowdown. Political conflicts were reflected in the frequent change in government during this period. Al-Iryani's government was too fragile and dependent on foreign assistance to jeopardize its relations with these allies. Finally, in June 1974, lack of confidence in the presidency of Al-Iryani was publicly expressed. The army moved in to take power and Al-Iryani boarded a plane for permanent exile.

Consequently, development projects for the infrastructure suffered from a lack of continuity. Projects were initiated and then stopped, according to which faction held power in government. Furthermore, development planning was concentrated in the major cities, since the government believed that it was essential to begin with building the central infrastructure. In the rural areas the provision of development projects was primarily hierarchical, reflecting the political importance of the village. A large number of rural people abandoned their land and migrated to the city in the hope of gaining more access to benefits that would improve their quality of life. Many men emigrated to Arab oil countries, which at the time were enjoying the benefits of the oil boom.

As a result, the Republican regime and the transformation process introduced new forms of exclusion. These exclusions were related to social and economic development policies. That is, as some citizens were receiving the benefits of social and economic development such as those in the major cities, others were being deprived. In addition, new social networks emerged based on economic status. They reflected a new social class consisting of the military groups that established positions of power, and a minority of technocrats. However, the old and new networks were not mutually exclusive. For example, the majority of the military had become incorporated from a tribal background. Hence, transformation by accommodation not only brought about the rise of dualism, but also embedded it into the political, economic, and social systems.

## 2. Transformation by social revolution: The People's Democratic Republic of Yemen

In November 1967, a left-wing civil nationalist group, the National Liberation Front (NLF), won independence from the British. It became known as the People's Republic of South Yemen (PROSY), and would be renamed the People's Democratic Republic (PDRY) in 1970. It was among the countries in the region that had experienced the longest period of colonialism.

In the engineering for independence, a social dimension emerged in the liberation struggle. Large numbers of poor peasants volunteered to serve in the guerilla army established by anti-colonial cadres. Deeb [1986, p. 454] explains that the impoverished conditions in both the economically backward provinces and the economically developed Aden (seen in the latter in largely urban working class) paved the way for the radical faction's unique social base, uniting the rural and urban areas under the banner of a Marxist ideology. This mass appeal emanated from the interest of the workers and poor peasants in a fundamental change in the existing systems of the social and economic order, whether in Aden or the countryside.

The old leadership in the hinterlands was destroyed with the colonial overthrow. Most of the sultans fled the country with their supporters. The

British political framework, the British-trained and the British influenced elites, were replaced by a radical movement to lead the country. Thus, space was cleared for the creation of a new social order.

External politics in the region, such as the ongoing civil war in North Yemen, also influenced the political idealogy of the revolutionary movement [Ismael & Ismael, 1986, p. 162]. For example, the involvement of the Saudis and Egyptians in neighbouring North Yemen's civil war symbolized different economic idealogies. The Saudis symbolized the elites, who supported preserving the traditional status quo, while the Egyptian Nasserism movement represented a popularized national movement promoting revolutionary programmes of social reform and social trans- formation. The end of the civil war in Yemen, and the accommodation of the traditional social order in the new Republic, did not impress the revolutionaries in the South, who were not interested in replacing the colonial leaders by their traditional elites.

As a result, South Yemen was to become the first and only country in the Middle East to adopt scientific socialism. However, what followed was an interim of political struggle for power within the NLF party and for leadership of the state. The competing groups in the NLF were divided into two main groups: radicals and moderates. These divisions reflected social class, political ideology, and personality conflicts. The radicals were composed of active cadres radicalized by the anti-colonial struggle. They were interested in the revolutionary transformation of society according to Marxist-Leninist ideology. Their mass support included the urban workers, the petite bourgeoisie in the provinces, and the poor peasants. They considered a socialist transformation a natural continuation of the liberation struggle. The moderates, on the other hand, were external cadres who were regarded as the revolutionary elite. They had not been exposed to the relationship between the colonial rule and the domestic social order. They won support of tribal elements and sections of the petite bourgeoisie in Aden [Deeb, 1986, p. 454]. This faction was headed by President Qahtan Al-Shaabi. Disagreement over foreign policy issues included, for example, the moderates' desire to resume relations with neighbouring countries in the region (particularly the oil-rich Arab states) and to encourage foreign investment to secure the critically-needed hard currency. The radicals wanted to take a more hard-line position by limiting their ties with other countries to the Soviet Union and other socialist states.

Despite overtones of the political idiom in these conflicts, there were also underlying personal conflicts. Individuals became identified with political positions, and past tensions were perpetuated within the ranks of the leadership [Ismael & Ismael, 1986, p. 77]. Patronage and nepotism was also noted in the Party and in the State system. Many of the revolutionary cadres who later became the political leaders were from the petite bourgeoisie. Leaders appointed their followers and relatives to positions of power. In times of political conflict, political leaders resorted to the traditional base of power. Thus, many political leaders maintained their regional allegiances and tribal patronage for support. By 1978, only 25 per cent of the Party delegates (125 out of 496) represented workers and cooperative peasants or fishermen [Deeb, 1986, p. 458].

The 1969 Corrective Step represented the overthrow of the moderates and the ascendancy of the radical socialists. However, the country continued to be plagued with political conflict, which was an impediment to transformation and to the social and economic development of the country.

## A. Social integration by institutionalization

Social integration in the PDRY was defined within the context of the transformation of society from a state of colonialism and semi-feudalism to a state of sovereignty and socialism. Thus, social integration was promoted through socialism and the ideas of establishing a collective unit where all citizens were treated as equals. This transformation was to be implemented by means of establishing an infrastructure that represented the socialist state ideology. The primary objective of these institutions was to unify society economically and socially. Various structures were established at different levels that would have the responsibility of overlooking the mobilization and participation of society.

At the head of these state institutions was the Politburo of the Party Central Committee. The Party was designed to ensure the ideological purity of the state in all its functions. The two principle tenets of the Party were democratic centralism and collective leadership. Thus, the leadership of the Party, as a collective unit, was to represent a safety barrier, to prevent the state from ever falling into the hands of an individual leader [Ismael & Ismael, 1986, p. 68]. Nonetheless, there were frequent tensions between the Party and state leaders over the implications of policy. For example, state officers were more pragmatic in their policy perspectives, since they had to deal directly with day-to-day aspects of domestic and international issues. In contrast, Party leaders took a more ideological position on policy issues confronting the state.

At the administrative level, each ministry had a branch in the governorate capitals and some had offices in the towns of the directorates (the units into which the governorates were subdivided). The aim was for Government to be able to extend its administrative apparatus throughout the country. Ideally, these government offices were to communicate information on policies to the people, and provide them with a place where they could go to obtain needed documents as well as assistance. However, a major problem from which these administrations suffered was weak management. This was attributed to the absolute shortage of trained personnel [Lackner, 1985, p. 100].

The Supreme People's Council was made up of members representing constituencies. Usually, the representatives were not from the area which they represented. Although this implied that the representatives would have less knowledge of the area's problems, it was also intended to disable the Council from reviving traditional networks and clientship with members seeing themselves as local lords. The Local People's Council (LPC), on the other hand, consisted of members who lived and worked in their constituencies and were considered in touch with the immediate problems of the localities for which they were responsible.

## B.  Social integration by means of economic and social development

The Party was responsible for overseeing planning for the economic and social development of the country. This included comprehensive planning aimed to mobilize human and economic resources in the interests of national integration and social and economic development. Development planning was to consist of regional planning.

The State's social and economic goals were to transform society from its traditional colonial structures to a modern state economy. However, the new leaders were confronted with an underdeveloped economy that consisted of a primitive agricultural sector and a large urban service sector left behind from the colonial regime, which had become dispensable post-independence. There was also a high dependency on imported goods, and the industrial sector was almost non-existent. Also, the withdrawal of the British included the withdrawal of naval installations in Aden, which had accounted for one-quarter of the GNP. This coincided with the closing of the Suez Canal, through which most of Aden's maritime business flowed. For example, the number of ships that called at the port of Aden dropped from 650 to 100 ships per month. This drastically cut port revenues, repair, and service charges, about one-fifth of the GNP [Ismail & Ismael, 1986, p. 8].

The new Government embarked on a series of radical measures that aimed to restructure, integrate and expand the national economy. The two most important policies that made significant economic and social changes were the Nationalization Law and the Agrarian Reform Law. The former included the nationalization of most foreign-owned enterprises. The objective of this law was to eliminate economic dependence, enhance national productivity, and establish a private sector to enable the State to control and direct the national economy. The State achieved its objective in having national control of the economy, but this was accomplished at a high price. The PDRY was cut off from the much-needed foreign exchange investment capital. There was also a plunge in expatriate remittances, which was mostly spent for house construction in the towns and villages. The negative effects of this policy finally made the State implement a gradual relaxation of investments policies. For example, restrictions that had been imposed on remittance deposits were given a concessionary rate of interest almost three times that offered to domestic depositors [Ismail & Ismael, 1986, p. 83]. As a result, remittances sent back to the country rose from $56 million in 1975 to approximately eight times that level a decade later. Expatriate remittances represented one-fifth of the GNP.

The Agrarian Reform Law had a significant impact in uprooting the semi-feudal social order in the hinterlands, and connecting rural people with the central government. Actually, land reform was initiated on 29 October 1970 by an uprising of hundreds of peasants who began arresting landlords and redistributing land. These takeovers soon spread throughout the country. The social significance of these popular uprisings is that they catalyzed the dissolving of the old social order. However, it was not until the Second Agrarian Reform Law in 1973, under the more leftist wing regime of Salem Rubayi Ali, that land reform was equitably implemented, primarily because at its earlier stages, President Al-Shaabi was not very supportive of this law. Restructuring of the agricultural system was along socialist lines. This law included the following important features: first, the lands of former protectorate officials and rural elites were confiscated without compensation. Second, landholding was limited to 20 *fedans* of irrigated land or 40 *fedans* of unirrigated land per individual and twice this amount per family (article 4).[15] In effect, most land distributed was 5 to 10 *fedans* per family [Deeb, 1986, p. 455]. Third, the law established agricultural cooperatives on confiscated land. People who had gained land through the reform law were encouraged to become members of the cooperatives. Fourth, private agricultural land was not prohibited, as long as peasant workers were not exploited. The Party wanted to ensure that private landowning farmers were guided to keep up with development in the agricultural sector. Nonetheless, the Party continued to attempt to persuade them to join cooperatives voluntarily. In addition, the State established

---

[15] One *fedan* is equivalent to 1.04 acres, or 0.42 hectares.

model farms to encourage peasants and cooperative societies to undertake collective work.

As a result, the Second Agrarian Reform Law abolished large-scale land ownership. Nearly half of the country's cultivated land was redistributed among some 25,778 landless or near landless families [Ismael & Ismael, 1986, p. 85].

The restructuring of the rural economy led to a relative improvement in the standard of living of rural workers. By 1977, the production of agricultural cooperatives made up 80 per cent of the total agricultural productivity of the country [Deeb, 1986, p. 455]. The social implications of this reform law included the cooperatives providing medical care and other social services that were not previously available. In spite of these significant improvements in the economic development of the agricultural sector, poverty was not eradicated in rural areas. Consequently, many peasants migrated to Aden or abroad in search of work.

Economic development in the urban areas (primarily Aden) focused on the severe problem of unemployment. Large investments were directed in labour-intensive development projects such as road building. The construction of the transportation and communication infrastructure was considered essential for national integration and long-term economic expansion.

Social development was designed to complement economic development that would expedite the eradication of structural poverty and inequality. Social policy was to provide an operational programme in areas such as health, safe drinking water, education, housing, and employment. Emphasis was put on expanding these services to rural areas where they were virtually non-existent. The State considered education the primary agent for the transition of society from its tribal structure to a modern economy state. The illiteracy rate at independence was 80 per cent, and 95 per cent among the rural population. There was a severe shortage of schools and teachers throughout the country. The State's commitment to education as a basis for social progress was indicated in its expenditure on education, which averaged 7.4 per cent of GDP, in contrast to the general 4.4 per cent of developing countries [World Bank, 1979, p. 74]. Some indicators of educational advance are provided in Table 1. On-the-job training programmes were conducted to upgrade the skills of the labour force. All public establishments also held literacy classes for their employees [Ismael & Ismael, 1986, pp. 120-121].

The social implications of labour polices included the eradication of unemployment, the minimization of income inequalities, and the elimination

**Table 1. Progress made in the education sector between 1966-1977**

|                             | 1966/67 | 1976/77 |
|-----------------------------|---------|---------|
| Number of schools           |         |         |
| primary                     | 329     | 976     |
| preparatory                 | 53      | 326     |
| secondary                   | 7       | 25      |
|                             |         |         |
| Number of teachers          |         |         |
| primary                     | 1 744   | 9 018[1] |
| preparatory                 | n.a.    | n.a.    |
| secondary                   | 165     | 532     |
|                             |         |         |
| Number of student enrolments |        |         |
| primary                     | 49 928  | 206 358 |
| preparatory                 | 11 583  | 43 410  |
| secondary                   | 2 992   | 10 940  |

*Note*:      [1] Primary and preparatory schools were combined into an eight-year programme.
*Source*:    Ministry of Education, 1979.

of exploitative labour relations. Law No. 14 included the legal framework for guaranteeing that labour benefit directly from economic growth, rather than through a trickle-down effect. The objective was to tie the welfare and quality of life of the working population to the state-run economy, eliminating tribal structures as the primary determinant of individual and collective social welfare [ibid., p. 124]. In section 13 of the Law, employees were also given the right to organize and join labour unions of their own free will, and the Confederation of Trade Unions was given the right to call a general strike. Unions were also empowered to set standards of working and living conditions for employees, and to participate in management decisions [ibid.].

Social policies also targeted underprivileged groups. According to the State, these groups were identified primarily as women and the Bedouins. Effecting change among these groups was particularly difficult because of the cultural and geographic barriers [ibid., p. 125]. Women had to overcome family and traditional beliefs in taking an active economic role in society. The state established the General Union of Yemeni Women with the objective of encouraging women to mobilize and participate in political, social and economic affairs. Molyneux [1982], in her study of the PDRY's policies on the position of women, found that state intervention and the implementation of a series of radical reforms contributed significantly to the improvement of the situation/position of women, making the PDRY one of the most advanced countries in the Middle East in this regard [ibid., p. 79].

The Bedouins represent about 10 per cent of the population and range over 67 per cent of the country's territory, which is semi-desert [Lackner, 1985, p. 112]. Economically, they survived on herding by very sparse grazing grounds. Although they produced one-third of the country's meat produce, the government recognized that the Bedouins' standard of living was minimally sustained. However, the geographic dispersion of the Bedouins made it very difficult to provide them with development benefits. State policy aimed to encourage the settlement of the Bedouins and their social and economic development. These objectives were implemented by means of the Bedouin Development Project. The project included the drilling of 52 boreholes by 1982 and the provision of facilities, which by their nature encourage settlements, such as basic shopping facilities and community development centres that provided a wide range of services — health units, education and training programmes, sewing, carpentry, carpet making, veterinary services, etc. A major component of this policy was the provision of schools; mainly boarding schools, which would allow parents to travel with their herds while their children were in school. Social surveys conducted in 1973 and 1981 showed a considerable improvement in the standard of living of the Bedouins. Literacy had increased from 25 per cent to 35 per cent; school attendance had increased from 2.3 per cent to 20 per cent for boys and from 0.5 per cent to 8 per cent for girls; Bedouins living in housing increased from 1 per cent in 1974 to 16 per cent in 1981; while the number of people involved in herding dropped from 90 per cent to 73 per cent [Lackner, 1985, pp. 112-113]. These indicators signified an increase in settled activities.

## C.  Political instability and economic crises

The internal political instability and the external economic decline in international oil prices were significant impediments to the social and economic development of the country and the transformation process. The State's main source of foreign currency was expatriate remittances and foreign aid. In the early 1980s the Arab oil boom, which had indirectly contributed to the PDRY's investments, sharply declined. The international oil glut reduced expatriate remittances and foreign aid from radical Arab allies such as Algeria, Iraq, Libya, and from other Arab aid agencies (such as the Kuwait Fund). Consequently, development projects were curtailed as a result of lack of financial resources. Rural areas were most affected by these cuts, and thus were excluded from full participation in development benefits. The lack of state presence in these areas allowed traditional economic and social ways of life to endure.

Social integration by means of economic development was short-lived as a result of the political crises and economic constraints. On 13 January 1986, violent fighting broke out between the Supreme People's Council (SPC) and the Yemen Socialist Party (YSP). After two weeks of bloody fighting and thousands of civilians killed, the YSP gained the upper hand, while the President Ali Nasser Mohammed sought refuge in North Yemen. By the end of the 1980s, the end of the Cold War, and the decline in foreign aid intensified the fragility of the political and economic system of the socialist regime. South Yemen was considered one of the poorest countries in the world. Furthermore, the ongoing conflicts in the State and Party contributed to the loss of credibility of the political leaders and their economic ideologies.

## D. Processes of exclusion

Colonialism and exploitation were instrumental in mobilizing and integrating society to overthrow the colonial regime, and in the rebuilding of a social system founded on revolutionary change. The establishment of state institutions based on socialist principles was a decisive force in setting in motion the transformation process. The State did succeed in establishing its authority in place of the colonial and traditional elites. However, the transformation process was never completed, and society remained in a state of transition and dualism.

An underlying factor for achieving complete transformation is the change in social behaviour, i.e. society's abandonment of traditional cultural practices. This was never fully accomplished in the PDRY. Paradoxically, political leaders continued to resort to tribal support during political conflicts. Tribal influence had been reduced but not abolished, since some leaders of tribal background maintained their loyalty to their clan. Thus, networks and social membership in sub-groups were maintained in the new socialist regime. Social relations played a role in attaining important positions in government. Consequently, political positions were in the hands of a defined minority of the petite bourgeoisie. Lackner [1985, p. 108], provides an example of how a Party member would rather marry his daughter to a suitor from his tribal relations or from a family of inherited status than to a suitor distinguished by his personal qualities. Hence, in spite of the Social Revolution of South Yemen, which abolished the institutions of the traditional social order, structural norms continued to influence social relationships. This indicates that change in social behaviour is very slow as a result of its built-in inertia. As a result, processes of exclusion embedded in structural norms continue to be witnessed in social behaviour and social relations, while new approaches to social relations develop very slowly. Perhaps if the PDRY had succeeded in establishing a stronger economy, it may have catalyzed the change in social attitudes and relations.

Processes of social exclusion were present in the state's economic development policies. In the urban areas, the State provided jobs for the working class; however, their status remained that of a "working class" [Deeb, 1986, p. 456]. These jobs possessed only horizontal mobility. This illustrates a different dimension of exclusion in the labour market, i.e. when people are employed, but not in jobs that enhance their economic well-being. According to the revolutionaries' ideology, the working class was to take a more active and equal role in governing the State. Instead, the working class remained a marginal political force under the socialist State.

Processes of social exclusion resulting from social and economic development policies were also evident in many rural areas. This was a result of the government's inability to extend development benefits to the entire country, because of its financial and technical constraints. As a result, as some people in some parts of the country were developing, others were trapped in a livelihood of poverty and deprivation.

In conclusion, the transformation of the PDRY was relatively more advanced than that of the YAR. This occurred mainly because the revolution overthrew the old social order, and established modern institutions to implement social and economic policies. However, this did not bring an end to traditional structural norms, which continued to be apparent in social behaviour. Yet both countries had factors in common that hindered their ability to achieve social integration and their complete transformation to modern economy States. These consisted of ongoing political instability; economic stagnation; and the fragility of the state's institutions, which did not have the dynamics to promote transformation, especially of rural society.

## III. The state of dualism:
## National integration and processes of exclusion

The unification of North Yemen and South Yemen on 22 May 1990 reinforced the government's concern and priority for social integration. However, the notion of integration was expanded to include the integration of people from two countries with different economic, political, and social institutions. The complexity of this endeavour included the integration of conflicting ideologies in these systems. For example, the new political system included religious, tribal, modernist, and socialist factions.

The government of the Republic of Yemen (ROY) declared itself a democratic State guided by the principles of Islam. Thus, religion was the common denominator that would unite the two societies. Another pragmatic step of the new regime was to establish a government based on a multi-party system. This was the first of its kind in the Middle East. The international community applauded this impressive movement. This move indicated two significant objectives of the ROY: first, sincere efforts to establish a democratic state; and second, a strategy of national integration based on accommodation, i.e. with all political factions represented in the political system.

Political slogans throughout the country echoed the importance of Yemen unity, one people, and the rights of all citizens to equal economic and social development. Many believed that unification would herald a new era of democracy and prosperity in Yemen. Instead, what followed was a series of external and internal political and economic crises that paralyzed the country.

## 1.  Barriers to social integration

Unification compounded the problems of social and economic development that were faced by each of the two countries before the unification. During this period of political transition, problems of poverty were exaggerated by internal and external political and economic factors. These factors can be summarized as follows.

First, South Yemen, the poorer of the two, made very little financial contribution to the unification process. North Yemen's limited resources had to be stretched further to support another 2 million people. As a result, the acquisition of basic needs became more difficult for some and totally unattainable for others.

Second, the breakout of hostilities on 5 May 1994 between the government and a seceded faction has undoubtedly had drastic effects on the economy of Yemen. The full effect of this war on the people's livelihood continues to unfold.

Externally, a few months after unification, the Gulf War broke out. The political stand taken by the ROY during the Gulf War offended many donor countries, especially the oil-rich Arab countries. The consequences were devastating to Yemen's economy. First, over one million emigrant Yemeni workers in the Gulf were forced to return to their country on very short notice. The State was not prepared to provide

**Table 2: Official development assistance[1]**

|  | 1987 | 1988 | 1989 | 1990 | 1991 | 1992 |
|---|---|---|---|---|---|---|
| **Bilateral** | 360.6 | 244.3 | 285.1 | 352.1 | 254.4 | 171.2 |
| of which: |  |  |  |  |  |  |
| Arab countries | 192.2 | 66.5 | 80.1 | 172.0 | 13.7 | 14.4 |
| Japan | 27.7 | 29.1 | 72.2 | 23.0 | 105.3 | 34.7 |
| Netherlands | 28.5 | 35.0 | 30.9 | 30.4 | 25.3 | 31.5 |
| Germany | 32.4 | 33.1 | 27.4 | 38.0 | 23.5 | 29.6 |
| France | 4.3 | 9.0 | 3.5 | 16.7 | 20.1 | 18.3 |
| USA | 45.0 | 27.0 | 40.0 | 43.0 | 21.0 | 13.0 |
| Denmark | 8.6 | 16.3 | 12.7 | 13.2 | 12.9 | 4.1 |
| UK | 10.4 | 12.6 | 10.6 | 9.9 | 9.3 | 9.9 |
| **Multilateral** | 131.7 | 134.4 | 150.8 | 123.2 | 121.2 | 135.0 |
| of which: |  |  |  |  |  |  |
| World Bank | 40.4 | 49.0 | 43.0 | 33.0 | 49.0 | 52.9 |
| Arab agencies | 43.6 | 38.8 | 42.6 | 29.0 | 25.5 | 33.8 |
| WFP | 18.5 | 19.3 | 27.0 | 21.0 | 15.1 | 9.4 |
| UNDP | 4.9 | 9.3 | 14.6 | 17.2 | 13.5 | 10.0 |
| **Total** | 492.3 | 378.7 | 435.9 | 475.4 | 366.0 | 306.1 |

Note:　　[1] Gross disbursements. Official development assistance is defined as grants and loans with at least a 25% grant element, provided by OECD and OPEC member countries and multilateral agencies.

Source:　　OECD, geographical distribution of financial flows to developing countries (cited from EIU, 1995).

housing, health care, employment and other social services for these emigrants. Their annual remittances which used to contribute approximately 400 million dollars to Yemen's GNP, were also lost. In addition, all aid from the oil-rich Arab countries was halted and aid from Western industrialized countries and international organizations was significantly curtailed (see Table 2). Shanty towns consisting of emigrant families sprouted in and around the major cities, schools became overcrowded, and unemployment rates soared.

## 2. Political instability and social exclusion

The present political tensions in Yemen reflect a complex web of traditional and modern structures that have become embedded in the system. This also reflects the impediments to the advancement of Yemen's transformation process. For instance, the multi-party system, in contrast to its objectives, has not paved the way for social transformation by citizen participation and integration from the sub-group level to an economic community level. Instead, the accommodation of different political parties that range from conservative tribal leaders to secular modernists under the guise of a modern system sustains the dualism. This political parties that range from conservative tribal leaders to secular modernists under the guise of a modern system sustains the dualism. This dualism is associated with a competition over power and protection of interests. At a social level, this dualism is sustaining divisions rather than integrating society. As a result of the ongoing political instability, the economic crisis is being prolonged, and thus people's standard of living is declining.

Since the end of the internal war (July 1994), the government has been pursuing efforts to normalize the situation in the country; the underlying objective has been national unity. This was exhibited in reasserting the YSP's participation in the government. However, there continues to be unresolved internal conflict in government. The YSP position, for example, is precarious and they therefore have kept a low profile. In the southern governorates, according to a World Bank report [1995], people believe they are being marginalized in the government's new plans for economic development. For example, the government's plans of the Aden's Free Zone project have been abandoned. The government, due to its financial constraints, has recently proposed that this project be carried out by private investments [ibid., p. 21]. Meanwhile, the Islah's base of support is expanding and many Yemenis fear a tilt in the balance of power towards the Islah's dominance in government. To a growing number of Yemenis, Islah's rhetoric appears simple and indigenous, since it re-asserts the role of Islam in state and society. It comes at a time when many Yemenis are disillusioned with the country's experiences of development and democracy, which are perceived as having contributed to fragmenting society, promoting social inequality, and leading to a decline in people's standards of living. Thus, the Islah party represents an alternative approach, founded on the principles of Islam that are familiar to all classes of society, and which consist of moral norms that stress social unity and equality. For others, their suspicion of the Islah party is based on the party's political Islamic ideology and its external financial support, which are tied to foreign political agendas not necessarily representing the interest of Yemeni society. This is reflected in the lack of homogeneity of this party. For example, its leader, Shaykh Abdullah Al-Ahmar, is backed by Saudi Arabia, and represents tribal dominance in the central government rather than a religious figure. Other important members are followers of the Muslim Brotherhood movement in Egypt, and the Muslim Brotherhood movement in Sudan. The party's activities have also included targeting poor groups by providing them with staple foods during Ramadan and assisting their young in getting married, which is usually a financial burden in Yemeni culture.[16] They attempt to provide a safety net to the poor in their efforts to recruit them to their political movement. Already, Islah's enhanced position in Government was noted in the confirmation of the Sharia'a as the sole source of the legal system in the Constitution and women being discouraged from pursuing careers [EIU, 1995, p. 26].

In the meantime, social sectors have also been under strain in their provision of social services as a consequence of the unstable political situation. International development projects play a significant role in supplementing government efforts at social and economic development. Unfortunately, development aid is not provided objectively. It is strongly tied to political agendas. Many international organizations have resumed their development projects after the end of the war (July, 1994). However, many of these projects have been downsized. In addition, the slow international economy has affected bilateral aid to the country. Hence, the provision of economic and social development is decreasing, and in turn processes of social exclusion are put into motion.

## 3.   Economic reform and social exclusion

Extreme cases of poverty, unemployment, and marginalized groups in society have become very visible in the country. Although the poverty line of Yemen is unknown, the livelihood of many people is obviously below any reasonable measure of poverty. Schools are witnessing a decline in student enrolments and a rise in student drop-outs, since education is becoming perceived as a commodity rather than a necessity among lower income groups in society. Medical care is becoming unreachable to many, especially in relation to the cost of medicine. The market economy is strained by a depreciated national currency; inflation is at an all-time high; and employment opportunities are becoming rare. As a result, the competition over limited resources has made social networks the dominant factor in social and economic participation.

As a consequence of the degenerating economic environment, the government, after strong recommendations from the World Bank, has adopted a structural adjustment policy. One objective of this policy is to remove state subsidies and promote privatization in order to stabilize the diminishing resources available to the government. According to the World Bank recommendations [1995], the government's economic reform programme is to include the following: (1) the removal of food subsides

---

[16] For example, the cultural wedding festivities should extend for at least three days. The Islah encourages group weddings to cut down wedding expenses, and at times mediates the dowry. They have also constructed a ceremony hall where wedding festivities can be held.

(this includes the wheat and wheat flour programme; (2) a freeze in government employment; (3) the encouragement of investment and an increase in domestic production; (4) the privatization of public sector industries and services such as state entities in transport (including airlines), banking, trading sectors, and tourism; and (5) the reform of the safety net programmes.

Although there is an urgent need for economic reform, some of the government's structural adjustment policies will have devastating effects on the poor and will promote their social exclusion. Policies such as a reduction in government employees are needed. The bloated civil service sector and the presence of "ghost" employees contributes to waste in the system. Although the repercussions of this policy will compound problems of unemployment, especially since civil servants represent 16 per cent of the labour force, in the long run the efficiency of the government bureaucracy may be enhanced and government expenses reduced. However, for this policy to be effective it must also be accompanied by the elimination of the prevalent problems of corruption and mismanagement in the system. The policy of privatization of some public sector entities may also help fuel private investment and economic activity. The World Bank has not recommended privatization of the education and health sector, and has stated the importance of their protection [World Bank, 1995, p. 24]. However, the Government is considering increasing charges for these services. An increase in the charge for schooling was implemented after unification, and this has already affected many families' ability to send their children to school. At a time when the problems of poverty are increasing, additional charges for social services will only contribute to further deprivations. The major threat to the poor in the structural adjustment programme, however, is represented in the latter two policies: the removal of subsidies and the reform of the present government's safety net programme. These two policies are inter-related, since food subsidies represent the major element of the government's safety net programme. During such economic hardships, safety nets are critical. In other words, Yemen's two main formal safety nets have been: (1) universal subsidies (the wheat and flour programme), which consist of the government providing the poor with inexpensive staple food items; and (2) the non-governmental organizations (NGOs) that have specifically concentrated on assisting the poor and socially disadvantaged. Thus, the removal of subsidies means the elimination of a major safety net. A social safety net is a set of programmes designed to assist the poor who have fallen below a socially acceptable living standard. According to the World Bank report, these programmes have not been sufficient to attack problems of poverty.

report, these programmes have not been sufficient to attack problems of poverty.

Ideally, safety nets should be established before the implementation of the structural adjustment programme, which consists of severe economic and social restructuring. However, as of the time this study was being prepared, no safety net programmes had been set up, nor even designed. Yet the removal of subsidies had been initiated. Data from many developing countries that have adopted the structural adjustment programme have indicated its disastrous social and economic consequences. For example, it has threatened the livelihood of the younger generations in society. Basic needs such as calorie intake have been unattainable for children in African and Latin American countries that have adopted a structural adjustment programme.[17] The government, however, should not take sole responsibility for its failure to prepare safety nets before the implementation of this economic reform programme. International organizations, particularly the World Bank, are also responsible for having failed to assist the government in preparing safety net programmes prior to the implementation of these economic reform policies. The World Bank is aware of the government's constraints in designing safety net programmes. A World Bank report explains that the difficulties in designing safety net programmes in Yemen lies in identifying and reaching the poor. For example, in urban areas, the existence of a large population employed in the informal sector makes it difficult to determine a person's income. In the rural areas, on the other hand, a large percentage of the poor reside in dispersed and unreachable villages. As a result, the implementation of economic reform without provisions for protecting the poor will undoubtedly endanger poor people's livelihoods.

In conclusion, societies in transition that have fragile social welfare institutions resort under such circumstances to their traditional groups in search of group solidarity. It is also under these situations that individuals who lack social membership in sub-groups are pushed out to the periphery of society. Thus, their exclusion is twofold: exclusion from government institutions that would provide them with social welfare; and exclusion from traditional sub-groups, which would provide them support and solidarity.

---

[17] UNICEF and the UN Economic Commission for Africa estimated that at least six million children under the age of five have died each year since 1982 as a result of structural adjustment policies that have included cuts in social spending on health and education.

## *IV. Conclusion*

The two Yemens' transformation from a state of primordial societies, to independent states with different political economies, and finally to one united country, demonstrates the way in which this society became engulfed in a state of transition and dualism. Each different political phase indicated why social integration was critical to the different political systems and their leaders. These attributes are pertinent in understanding social integration and social exclusion. The political history of Yemen also indicates the importance of considering the role of the State in processes of social exclusion. This is primarily because processes of exclusion are embedded in the notions of social membership and citizenship. The transformation of society into a modern economy state is contingent on the transformation of social membership from a sub-group level to the national level. For this reason political leaders play a principal role in promoting social integration. Economic and social development are the major incentives in poor developing countries. The fragility of the modern political system and its institutions challenges political leaders' efforts at national integration, and helps sustain the dynamics of traditional structural norms. The two major factors that promote processes of exclusion are the social order and national development policies. As a result, processes of exclusion are dualistic in nature, involving both those that are related to structural norms, and those that are embedded in national development policies. Different groups are excluded as a result of one or both of these factors. Thus, as certain groups in society advance socially and economically by gaining access to development benefits, such as education, others are left behind in poverty and a process of social exclusion.

Furthermore, Yemen's experience of transformation from a primordial to a modern state also highlights the most predominant new dimensions of exclusion: basic needs, employment, and social and political representation. The last dimension became more obvious under the ROY. The promotion of democracy, in which all citizens have an equal right to social and political representation, and yet certain groups remain unable to obtain effective representation, made this dimension of exclusion more obvious.

# Chapter 3

## Traditional structural norms and new dimensions of exclusion

The overview of Yemen's political history and its experience of social integration and economic development indicates how dual processes of social exclusion have emerged. During the transition of society, structural norms continue to play a role in enabling some groups' access to resources and services while excluding others. Simultaneously, new exclusions have been emerging as a result of the political economy's failure to deliver equitable access to social and economic development. This chapter briefly summarizes the main social strata in the traditional social order and examines three important new dimensions of exclusion.

### I.  The traditional social order

Traditionally, genealogy and access to land are important structural norms that determine social stratification, political and economic power in Yemen [Shaher, 1991, p. 218; Al-Sharjaby, 1986, p. 55]. These norms also reflect structural processes of inclusion and exclusion. The economic status of the individual is secondary to genealogy. In the major cities these norms are slowly changing with the emergence of a market economy society. These traditional social norms, however, continue to be dominant among the rural population.

In Western capitalist societies, social status is largely based on economic well-being. This reflects the transformation from a primordial society based on family and kinship to a society that is based on individualism, meritocracy and production. In the southern governorates, a similar transformation was prompted by the political-economic ideology of the previous socialist regime. This transformation, however, was not completed. Traditional structural norms continued to prevail in the countryside. In the northern governorates, transformation was initiated by the recruitment of young Western educated Yemenis into government and the rise of an entrepreneur class.

Although new socio-economic groups are emerging such as the military, and the entrepreneurs, Yemen's modern society continues to be influenced by its traditional social hierarchy. Thus, traditional social stratification defines the overall social order. The different social strata are:[18]

1.  The *sayyids*: These are the traditional elites who are direct descendants of the Prophet Mohammed. From the ninth century until the twentieth century, Yemen was a traditional Islamic state, and the *sayyids* were the only legitimate candidates for the Imamate position. Professionally, they functioned as government administrators and scholars. Although some of the *sayyids* held important positions in government or were wealthy landlords, many had more modest economic means. Nonetheless, they were still sought after to mediate in tribal disputes in recognition of their religious knowledge and their neutral stance (*sayyids* have no tribal affiliations). Thus, the *sayyids* had social, religious and political statue. After the 1962 Revolution, the political influence of the *sayyids* was curtailed as a result of their previous association with the old regime of the Hamid al-Din.

2.  The *Qadis* (Judges): These are highly respected scholars of Islamic law (the *Sharia'a*). During the Imamate regime, the *qadi*'s allegiance, in terms of consummatory values, was to the institution — i.e. the Imamate — rather than to a particular Imam. Their religious expertise and the administrative positions they held in the central government in the provinces endowed them with a high social status. After the 1962 revolution, *qadis* were integrated into the state's judicial system and other important positions in government.

3.  Tribal *shaykhs* and landlord *shaykhs*: The difference between the two lies in their social organization. A tribal *shaykh*'s prestige is based on tribal allegiance and military strength. Tribal *shaykhs* typically function as heads of independent entities. Both the Imams and the Republican government have had a precarious relationship with the tribal *shaykhs*,

---

[18] Studies relating to Yemen's social hierarchy vary, especially in regard to describing the lower strata. See Shaher [1991, pp. 217-220].

especially those in the northern highlands.[19] On the one hand, the political leaders depend on tribal military assistance during times of internal conflict and/ or external threat. On the other hand, the tribal *shaykhs* and their followers constitute a major force to be reckoned with. The *shaykhs* vary in terms of power and influence. Where one *shaykh* may have influence over 1,000 people, another may have power over 100,000 people (a multi-tribal *shaykh*). In addition, there is an omni-tribal *shaykh*, who carries the title *shaykh-al-mashaykh* (*shaykh* of all *shaykhs*). The latter two types of *shaykh* are usually members of government.

Landlord *shaykhs*, unlike tribal *shaykhs*, were given the title of *shaykhdom* in recognition of their economic status as wealthy landlords. The landlord *shaykh* is usually from the most affluent family in the district in terms of land, family reputation and prestige. A landlord *shaykh*'s power was based on his role as a government satellite for collecting taxes and overseeing the enforcement of law and order in the countryside [Shaher, 1991, p. 225]. Both tribal and landlord *shaykhs* oversee the entire activities in the villages, act as intermediaries in case of village or personal conflict, receive government officials, and act as government coordinators. The *shaykh* represents the district, and is the treasurer. He receives a monthly or yearly budget and enjoys all privileges due to a supreme command individual. Both tribal and landlord *shaykhs'* powers were reinforced in the North by their integration into the central government after the establishment of the YAR. *Shaykhs* at present, hold positions in the Council of Representatives.

4.  Tribes: They trace their genealogy to the indigenous Southern Arabian tribes descendants of Qahtan the son of the prophet Hud. This was the great pre-Islamic civilization of the Himyarite dynasty. While tribes in Arabia are often thought of as nomadic, Yemeni tribes are predominantly peasants and herdsman, as well as fighters. The tribes occupy the poorer semi-arid part of the country in the north and the east. In tribal regions of Yemen's northern and central highlands, the livelihood of the tribes depends on dry farming for subsistence and thus they are not particularly wealthy [Dresch, 1989, p. 9]. Their staple crops include sorghum, wheat, and barley. In the more arid eastern regions, there is more reliance on herding of sheep and goats. Each

---

[19] Tribal *shaykhs* in South Yemen lost most of their influence after the establishment of the PDRY.

tribe functions more or less like a small nation with its own boundaries, grazing grounds, wells, market towns, allegiances and enemies. They have their own unwritten laws and usages, called *urf* that are passed down from one generation to the next. They also have their own courts for settling water, boundary and other internal disputes. Thus, each tribe's loyalty and allegiance is devoted first and foremost to its tribal clan, religion, and community. The Imams of Yemen depended on tribal military strength for their survival. Also, historically, tribes would not indulge in what they considered lowly urban activities such as trade or manufacturing. However, in the last two decades, their lack of ability to sustain their livelihood on subsistence agriculture has led a significant number of tribes to emigrate to urban centres or abroad, and take up employment in jobs that require minimal or no skills, due to of their lack of training and illiteracy. A significant number of tribes have joined the army.

5.    The peasants: The peasants reside on richer agricultural land outside tribal territory to the west and south. Their tribal characteristics gradually dissolved as a result of the Rasulid dynasty (1174 AD-1454 AD). The Rasulid administered most of the south and coastal region through a sophisticated bureaucracy. Civil servants replaced the chiefs of tribes and tribal groupings. Social identity gradually became associated with geography rather than kinship and clan. Codes of customary law eventually disappeared, and the ability to organize coalitions of broad scope in pursuit of a specific common objective was lost [Stookey, 1974, p. 252]. Most peasants do not own the land but work on the property of the landlord *shaykhs*. Their economic situation is totally dependent on the landlord *shaykh* who has complete authority over agricultural productivity and marketing. Unlike the highland tribes, they do not have an interdependent relationship with their *shaykh*.

6.    Service-oriented professions: this includes a wide array of professions ranging from commerce and trade, to technicians, butchers, barbers, musicians, etc. Traditionally, people who were involved in such urban types of occupations went about unarmed. They were considered not to have a common descent group to support them nor did they control any land. Consequently, they were considered weak and were referred to as *masakin* or *du'afa*. More recently, professions in commerce and trade are gaining more social recognition. This is a direct result of two factors: (i) the involvement of the highland tribes in this economic activity; and (ii), the emergence of a market economy that is changing

people's attitudes, particularly in the cities. Thus, this group reflects social change in society as a result of economic development. Those that have become more affluent are breaking into the traditional elite circles. Furthermore, this reflects new patterns of social relationships based on economic status rather than on social status.

7.   The *akhdam* are at the very bottom of the social hierarchy. Their low social status and lack of economic participation are hereditary. The adverse combination of an unknown genealogy and employment in the most menial jobs have placed them on the fringes of society.[20]

## II.  *Exclusion from the labour market*

Yemen's economy is characterized by a low level of domestic industry; a low level of agricultural productivity; an aggressive informal sector; and a high percentage of unskilled workers in the labour force. The Gross Domestic Productivity (GDP) has strengthened as a result of a rapid increase in oil production (which increased by 56 per cent in 1994 as a result of the exploitation of new oil fields). On the other hand, the political crises which the Republic of Yemen has experienced since the early 1990s have traumatized the economy, and external sources that had fuelled much of the economy in the 1970s and 1980s (including emigrant remittances, foreign aid, and borrowing) have been seriously curtailed.

Emigrant remittances contributed over half of foreign-exchange income in the recent past, but the return of almost one million emigrant workers and their dependents from the Arab Gulf states as a consequence of the government's political stance during the Gulf War in 1992, meant the loss of this important external source. Current industries include crude oil production and petroleum refining, small-scale production of cotton textiles and leather goods, food processing, fishing, handicrafts, small aluminum products, and cement. But the economy is primarily dominated by a domestic service sector, mainly government and trade, which contributes half of the GDP. The Government sector includes oil export, which has become Yemen's major export commodity since 1988 and now generates 85 per cent of the earnings. The second largest sub-sector is wholesale and trade. Yemen's patterns of investment and consumption are heavily import reliant. This is a result of the weak local production, and reflects society's high level of consumerism.

---

[20] More information is provided on this group in Chapter 4.

**Table 3: Labour force composition, 1990[1]**

|  | Employees | % of total labour force | Female workers as % of sectoral total |
|---|---|---|---|
| Agriculture | 1 615 320 | 62.0 | 40.7 |
| Mining & quarrying | 7 323 | 0.3 | 0.9 |
| Manufacturing | 105 482 | 4.0 | 15.3 |
| Power & water | 17 663 | 0.7 | 3.1 |
| Construction | 144 941 | 5.6 | 0.6 |
| Wholesale | 184 915 | 7.1 | 3.7 |
| Transport & communications | 104 459 | 4.0 | 0.6 |
| Commerce | 10 198 | 0.4 | 9.9 |
| Public & personal services | 414 621 | 15.9 | 3.2 |
| **Total** | 2 604 922 | 100.0 | 26.7 |

*Note*:    [1] The data refers only to the active labour force employed and not to the total labour force.
*Source*:    Ministry of Planning & Development, 1992.

The agriculture and fishing sector generates one-fifth of the GDP, but employs almost two-thirds of the labour force (see Table 3). In 1993, agriculture accounted for 26 per cent of the GDP and 70 per cent of the labour force in the northern governorates, and 17 per cent of the GDP and 45 per cent of the labour force in the southern governorates [EIU, 1994, p. 378]. Agricultural output is concentrated in cereals, fruits and vegetables, which are cultivated primarily for domestic production, but production does not meet local demand, and it is necessary to supplement grain supply by imports of 1.5 million tons, which is equivalent to twice the domestic production. Several factors restrain more advanced development of the agricultural sector, particularly:

(a) *Problems of water supply.* Although development efforts have concentrated on providing water systems to rural areas, a large portion of agriculture remains dependent on rainwater. This has affected rural migration and the abandonment of land, especially in the highlands, which is a major region for agricultural production. Other problems include the mismanagement and over-exploitation of water supply, mainly by the private pumping of water reserves, which threatens the country's water supply.

(b) *Land ownership.* This includes several issues such as the fragment-ation of land ownership and the concentration on subsistence agriculture rather than commercial production. This reflects the low income level of the majority of Yemen's agrarian society that has neither the financial nor the technical resources to make this transformation. In general, private investment is lacking in the agricultural sector. Furthermore, after unification and privatization of state land in the South, competing claims over land have emerged, especially in the fertile Governorate of Hadramawt. This has deterred some private investments in this region that were initiated by affluent emigrants after unification.

(c) *The dominance of qat production.* Due to high local demand and its low maintenance, it threatens the expansion of other agricultural products.[21]

As the country proceeds in its efforts to transform the economy from one based on agriculture subsistence to a market economy, changes in patterns of employment inevitably result. Concentrations of poor, illiterate and unskilled individuals in rural areas are at the front line of exclusions from the labour market. They have been squeezed out of their traditional livelihoods and have no avenues to allow them to re-insert themselves into the modern economy.

Exclusion from the labour market is worsened by the following:

*(a)* a slow economy and a high rate of unskilled labour;

*(b)* lack of investment in industrial and modern sector activities;

*(c)* conventional development planning, that is, industries, services, and utilities are concentrated in the major cities and their outskirts;

*(d)* the use of capital-intensive techniques that have led to an increase in productivity with no additional employment opportunities;

*(e)* lack of training programmes that provide unskilled and illiterate labourers with skills that fulfill the needs of the economy.

Access to the urban labour market in developing countries is influenced by three factors: education, gender, and patronage [Gugler, 1988, p. 64]. This also applies to Yemen's urban labour market. Rural/urban migrants depend on their kin in urban centres to assist them with employment and provide them with housing. Barriers to the labour market result from lack of one or more of these factors. More recently, economic constraints and demographic shifts have had a major effect on social networks and employment opportunities.

The lack of equitable economic development in rural areas has forced many to emigrate in search of employment in the major cities or

---

[21] The impact of *qat* on Yemen's economy is discussed in the following paragraphs.

abroad. However, their ability to participate in the labour market fluctuates according to the state of the economy. In the 1970s, there was a shortage of Yemeni manual labourers because many had emigrated to Arab oil states. This led to a major increase in the import of labourers, particularly from Asia. Expatriate workers were hired to fill jobs in all sectors of the economy. By the mid-1980s, the slowing of the international economy forced many Yemeni workers, especially those in the Arab Gulf states, to return. However, these returning workers found themselves in competition with expatriate workers. The political and economic crises of the 1990s compounded the situation even further. Currently the country has a glut of semi-skilled and unskilled workers.

The size of the labour force in Yemen has increased from approximately 2.6 million in the year 1988 to 3.5 million in 1991. This translates into an average annual growth rate of 9.9 per cent, which is three times the growth rate of the population [MPD, 1992, p. 103]. This rapid increase in the size of the labour force is a direct consequence of the Gulf War and the influx of large numbers of Yemeni workers returning from neighboring Gulf countries. It has resulted in high levels of unemployment. It is estimated that 23.3 per cent of the labour force was unemployed in 1990, and that in 1994 this rose to 40 per cent [EIU, 1995].

According to the Employment Law (1970, Article 10), employers may not employ expatriates before ensuring that there are no unemployed Yemenis registered in the employment offices who are suitable for the job [MLA, 1991]. Companies and employers that are permitted to employ non-Yemeni technicians must appoint Yemeni assist-ants to these technicians. These assistants are supposed to work side by side with the expatriate technicians so that they can eventually replace the expatriate workers when their work permit expires (Article 25). These entitlement, however, have not been effective in providing employment rights or opportunities for Yemeni labourers. For example, big hotels in the major cities (particularly Sana'a and Aden) continue to import hundreds of expatriate workers who are paid in hard currency. Hotel managers, who are also usually expatriates, argue that there are no Yemenis capable of performing this work. Statistics show, however, that many of the returnees worked in service-oriented professions while abroad. Many companies and industries feel more comfortable about hiring expatriate workers. Yemenis are also not being employed as training assistants. Thus, the private sector has not played a responsible role in alleviating problems of unemployment of Yemeni labourers.

Open unemployment demonstrates exclusion from the labour market. However, exclusion can also be within the labour market. This applies to labourers who can only find casual work or employment in menial jobs. In this case, labourers are confined to poorly-paid and low-skilled jobs. Rodgers [1994, p. 10] explains that the underlying issue in this case is a dualization process. On the one hand, there are "bad jobs" with easier access but where poverty is concentrated; and on the other hand, there are "good jobs" which provide a degree of security and acceptable working conditions, yet have restricted access. Hence, there are different levels of exclusion, so it is possible to be included in the labour market and at the same time excluded from the "good jobs" in the labour market.

In Yemen only 23 per cent of the active labour force is in the formal sector. A major characteristic of the labour force is the high level of semi-skilled and unskilled workers. Nineteen per cent of the total labour force are white-collar workers and 81 per cent are blue-collar workers. This distribution of the labour force is influenced by a number of factors, such as the rural-urban distribution of the population, the lack of industrial and modern sector activities, the high illiteracy rates (67 per cent), and the low level of education and training among the labourers (4 per cent).

According to a World Bank study [1992], the private sector employed an estimated 725,000 employees in 1990 (*less than* the number of emigrant workers who returned during the Gulf War crisis). Nearly 11 per cent of those in the private sector were employed in various types of industrial activities. The study concluded that the use of capital-intensive techniques has led to an increase in productivity, but no additional employment opportunities were generated. This study pointed out a general decline in employment opportunities in the private sector. The increase in job opportunities was primarily in the informal sector and in traditional agricultural and fishing sectors. This study attributed the decline in the growth of the private sector to administrative procedures and restrictions of the government and its laws and regulations that limited expansion.

The informal sector consists mainly of Yemen's underground economy, which is unrecorded. The two major economic activities are smuggling and the *qat* trade. These unrecorded activities have a serious impact; they distort the data of private sector activities and of the state of the economy in general.

Smuggling primarily consists of the trade of consumer imported goods. Most of these transactions take place along the Saudi borders and ports along the Red Sea. The commodities range from stereos to foreign cars and trucks. This activity is primarily controlled by the tribes who take advantage of their territorial borders with Saudi Arabia. The government has difficulty controlling these activities because its authority is weak outside the urban centres; it also wishes to avoid conflict with the tribes, who regard themselves as nearly autonomous.

Qat is a mild narcotic shrub whose leaves are chewed as a stimulant, and this activity takes place from after lunch until the call for evening prayers among Yemenis from all socio-economic classes. Qat is one of the highest consumer products and thus plays a pivotal role in employment, production, marketing and consumption patterns. However, all these activities are conducted in the informal market and are unrecorded. The scarce data available were noted in the Yemen Times, which provided some assessments of the qat sector [cited from EIU, 1995, p. 51]. It reported that in 1992 the value added by the qat sector was equivalent to 25 per cent of the GDP. The annual output of the shrub was 250,000 tons; least one-quarter of irrigated agricultural land was used for qat production; and it employed almost 50,000 people, almost 20 per cent of the labour force.

## III. Exclusion from basic needs

The population of the Republic of Yemen was estimated at 11.2 million, unevenly spread throughout the country (see Table 4) [MPD, 1992].[22] In 1992, Yemen's resident population was 75 per cent rural and 25 per cent urban. In 1994, it was estimated that the rural population had decreased to 62 per cent, and the urban population had increased to 38 per cent. These changes indicate the continuing pattern in rural-urban migration, and also the re-location of returnee migrants. The major urban centres, which account for more than half the urban population, are Sana'a, Taiz, Aden, Taiz, Ibb, and Hodiedah. The country has a high population growth rate of 3.5 per cent (1994), and it is estimated that 52.5 per cent of the population is under 15 years old of age.

The unfavourable ranking of Yemen in the human development index is a result of high illiteracy (62 per cent), high mortality of infants and children under five (118/1000 live births), high level of fertility (7.3), and high maternal mortality. In addition, this ranking reflects the poor standards of health services, electrification, housing, tapped water and sewerage

---

[22] This is made up of the population of 9 million of the previous Yemen Arab Republic, and 2.2 million of the People's Democratic Republic.

**Table 4: Estimated population, 1990**

| Age group | Number | % of total |
|---|---|---|
| 0 - 14 | 5 920 630 | 52.5 |
| 15 - 64 | 4 986 970 | 44.2 |
| 65+ | 371 850 | 3.3 |
| **Total** | 11 279 450 | 100.0 |
| of which: urban | 4 258 420 | 37.8 |

*Source*: Central Statistical Organization, Statistical yearbook.

**Table 5: Education statistics, 1989-90**

| | Northern governorates | | Southern governorates | | Total | |
|---|---|---|---|---|---|---|
| | Primary | Secondary | Primary | Secondary | Primary | Secondary |
| Schools | 6 960 | 462 | 1 039 | 61 | 7 999 | 523 |
| Pupils | 1 487 252 | 86 760 | 339 991 | 33 276 | 1 827 243 | 120 039 |
| of which female | 406 881 | 10 904 | 112 396 | 10 588 | 519 287 | 21 492 |
| Teachers | 30 321 | 2 374 | 12 406 | 1 730 | 42 717 | 4 104 |
| of which non-Yemeni | 19 046 | 1 723 | — | — | 19 046 | 1 723 |
| Ratios pupils per teacher/per total pupils (%) | 49 | 37 | 27 | 19 | 43 | 29 |
| Non-Yemeni teachers/ total teachers (%) | 62.8 | 72.6 | n/a | n/a | 44.6 | 42 |

*Source*: Central Statistical Organization, Statistical yearbook.

facilities, low skill levels and an undiversified labour force structure. These indicators underscore the urgent need for the provision of basic needs to provide an acceptable standard of living.

Basic needs represent goods and services essential for improving the quality of life. A large portion of society continues to be deprived of these services. Some indicators of provision of health and education services are given in Tables 5 and 6. It is estimated that health services are only accessible to 40 per cent of the total population [MOH, 1994]. Also, only 19 per cent of the total population in the age group 5-19 years are enrolled in formal education [MPD, 1992, p.113].[23]

---

[23] The Ministry of Planning and Development (MPD) uses this percentage only as a general indicator, since it is difficult to establish an accurate estimate of enrolment percentage because many of those in school are above this age group.

**Table 6: Health**

|  | Northern governorates | Southern governorates | Total |
|---|---|---|---|
| Doctors | 1 810 | 898 | 2 708 |
| Dentists | 109 | 35 | 144 |
| Pharmacists | 133 | 55 | 188 |
| Hospitals | 42 | 32 | 74 |
| Health centre & primary health-care units | 906 | 398 | 1 304 |
| Hospital beds | 4 488 | 3 482 | 7 970 |
| Health centre beds | 1 342 | 579 | 1 921 |
| **Ratios** |  |  |  |
| Head of population: |  |  |  |
| per doctor | 4 546[1] | 2 047[2] | 4 165[3] |
| per hospital | 195 918[1] | 57 445[2] | 152 425[3] |

*Notes*:  [1] Based on 1986 census of the YAR. [2] Based on 1988 census of PDRY. [3] Based on 1990 Ministry of Planning and Development projection.
*Source*:  Central Statistical Organization.

Basic needs deprivation appears in different guises. First, exclusion of some groups from basic needs can be explained by a simple supply and demand equation. The Government acknowledges its responsibilities; however, its ability to provide basic social services has been constrained by various interdependent factors, mainly the State's financial limitations. This problem has been compounded by the decline in external aid, rapid population growth rate, and the overall stagnant economy. Technical limitations also limit the effectiveness of the State's efforts in social provisioning. This includes shortages of physicians, nurses, teachers, and other professionals, who are concentrated in the major cities, and a poorly developed infrastructure (lack of paved roads, school buildings, hospitals, electricity, etc.). Second, even in situations where basic services are available, people are deprived of these services by their inability to pay for them, especially where opportunity costs are concerned. This is particularly evident in education and health. For example, although free education is guaranteed by the State, the income sacrifices demanded of the poor to pay for related expenses (textbooks, registration fees, clothing, etc.) are such that their children are more likely to be excluded from schooling. Similarly, the inability to pay for medicine excludes the poor from adequate health care.

In the past, deprivations of basic needs may have gone unrecognized by some. More recently, exposure of the population to the mass media and other sources of information has alerted them to the importance of basic needs such as education, health care, safe drinking water, and proper nutrition. Their deprivation of these services has become more acutely felt since they now realize the importance of these services and feel that they and their children are being excluded from a chance to improve their livelihood. Although the state realizes that providing its citizens with basic services is fundamental for human resource development of the country, its inability to meet these responsibilities is eroding public confidence in its effectiveness.

## IV. Exclusion from social and political representation

Public institutions, agencies, and social organizations provide citizens access to their government. They are channels for citizens to voice their grievances, needs, and requests from government. People's demand for education, health care, training, credit, and other means of the productive process itself represent some of the basic goods and services particularly significant to lower income groups in society. The presence of public or private institutions to represent their demands is essential. Effective representatives should demand, negotiate and lobby on behalf of their constituents in attaining these rights. Inversely, the lack of such representation deprives people from their social rights to political participation. The problem of lack of social and political representation impedes the establishment of a "collective consciousness" and the "social contract".

Exclusion from social and political representation is an issue closely associated with the issue of access to social membership at the national level. Political and social institutions that are accessible to citizens are essential for the integration of transitional developing societies. It is through these institutions that the notion of citizenship is promoted. They also advance the social transformation process by shifting loyalties from the sub-group level to the national level. As a result, citizens would no longer need to depend on social relationships such as tribal leadership and networks to have access to resources and services.

Shortly after unification, the Government of the ROY, in an effort to promote public participation and representation, allowed the organization of political parties. By 1992, there were about 45 political parties. However, many of these political parties remain strongly influenced by the traditional social order and networks of power.[24] Political affiliation is based more on

---

[24] There is a 301-seat Parliament composed of 159 members of the Shura Council, 111 from the Supreme People's Assembly and 31 representatives nominated by the President. Political pluralism and freedom of expression were significant steps towards the enhancement of democracy by the new Government post-unification [HRW, 1992, p. 4].

patronage and personal relationships than ideology [HRW, 1992, p. 13]. Political parties, however, have not improved poor citizens' participation and representation, basically because the notion of participation in political parties, democracy, and political pluralism are concepts that are familiar only to the educated minority. The poor and disadvantaged, for example, are unaware of how to organize or to utilize political parties to represent their needs and demands. The combination of their poverty and illiteracy is a major barrier to information, organization, and participation in the political process. Thus, poor groups do not consider the emergence of political parties a solution to their problems of deprivation from basic needs or employment. Consequently, traditional social structures are reinforced. For example, traditional political forces are concentrated in the northern and eastern governorates. These traditional social institutions, especially the more powerful tribes, continue to play an important role in providing political representation. Those outside these traditional social institutions face monumental barriers in attaining their social rights since strong social networks are needed at all levels to process social demands. In the southern and urban regions, tribal links are weaker and, although the state's authority is more widely recognized there are competing power conflicts, such as those between religious political groups and educated urban technocrats. In these areas, access to representation is based on networking among socio-economic equals. Consequently, as individuals and groups descend on the socio-economic scale so do their privileges and citizen's rights.

An important prerequisite for public participation and representation is the presence of a network of social institutions. This is essential for processing the influx of participation and mass demands. However, in Yemen, these institutions are not well established and do not cover the entire country, basically because the functions of these institutions have been stretched after unification without additional managerial organization, technical and financial support. The influx of citizen participation creates strains on the existing institutions which are not yet prepared to process mass demands. The lack of effective response from the institutions, in turn, leads to wide feelings of apathy towards the state.

Unions represent another means for citizen participation and representation. Prior to unification, the South had many active unions to represent different groups. Although unions were never really effective in influencing central policy they did, however, provide services to their members [Lackner, 1985, p. 100]. For example, the Peasant's Union organized literacy and other training classes, and resolved problems of peasants in cooperatives. The General Union for Yemeni Workers' responsibilities included overseeing the working conditions of workers, and protected their members' interests in matters such as salaries and benefits. The Youth Union, which also had a children's branch, organized summer camps, sports, and week-end outings. This Union was closely associated with the Student Union which was concerned with problems of students in the country and students studying overseas. Post unification, the role of unions is still not clear. The Union of Yemeni Women, which used to exist only in the South, was expanded to represent women from the North. This Union has been active in providing an independent panel for the discussion of women's rights.

Non-government organizations (NGOs), local and foreign, play an important role in targeting deprived groups, and providing them with social services such as literacy programmes, primary health care, and training in income-generating skills. However, these activities do not include social and political representation. NGOs work at a grassroots level and are well aware of the problems that different disadvantaged groups encounter. In the last few years, the number of local NGOs has increased significantly. The Ministry of Insurance and Social Affairs has supported local NGOs by making yearly financial contributions to them. International and bilateral donors have also provided them with financial and technical support. Unfortunately, most NGOs are concentrated in the cities and the larger villages. A few have tried to extend their activities to remote villages. However, in most cases, by the time the resources (financial and technical) reach these areas they usually are not sufficient to meet the great demand. Another factor that prohibits the expansion of more NGOs are government regulations concerning the establishment of NGOs. These include registration, fund raising, and other cumbersome operational activities [World Bank, 1995, p. 22-23]. NGOs can help government identify marginalized groups in society. They can also assist marginalized groups in educating them about their social rights and helping them organize. Thus, NGOs can be effective agents in linking government to poor excluded groups in society.

Currently, social or political organizations that encourage public participation, particularly among the poor, are lacking. Prior to unification, both the North and the South had social organizations that were based on grassroots participation. The successes and failures in both cases provide useful information that could be employed in future efforts at providing social and political participation and representation for the disadvantaged groups in society. The following paragraphs summarize the experiences of these social organizations. More emphasis is placed on North's experience with cooperatives, since their initiation was completely independent from the government.

As a response to the weakness of the central government of the YAR in providing services to rural areas in the early 1970s, local village communities organized and formed cooperative organizations to develop their own infrastructure. This included the construction of roads, water systems, schools, and health centres. The cooperative movement began in the southern Governorate of Taiz, which was the home base of the majority of immigrants, and affluent merchants and landlords. The northern Governorates of al-Jawf, Marib, and Sa'adah maintained their strong tribal allegiances. Cooperatives spread throughout the country and by 1975 there were 164, compared to 28 in 1973 [Piepenburg, 1992, p. 56]. These cooperatives, known as Local Development Agencies (LDAs), were funded by private donations, the *zakat*, and remittances. Local material and expertise were utilized. Planning and implementation of communal development projects were done with the utmost efficiency, since the projects represented people's needs and utilized their own money. The Ministry of Local Administration in 1991 stated that cooperative projects cost 40 per cent to 50 per cent less than those implemented by government [cited from Al-Saiidi, 1992, p. 57]. At a social level, the spirit of cooperation transcended traditional boundaries of social class in the villages. Politically, it fostered a spirit of democratic behaviour and nation building.

The sporadic rise of LDAs presented a challenge and opportunity to the former government of the YAR. On the one hand, the government had the desire to exercise some control over these communal organizations. On the other hand, LDAs represented an apparatus for state penetration to the countryside. Thus, by having control over the LDAs, the state would be able to have a strong local presence without acquiring the heavy financial and administrative burdens associated with building an entirely new institutional structure [Chaudhry, 1989, pp. 114-115]. As a result, Law No. 12 of 1985 defined the re-organization of the cooperatives. Fundamentally, it transferred the responsibility and power to the provincial governors. The LDAs, whose name was also changed to Local Council for Cooperative Development (LCCD), were to coordinate their projects and activities with the government represented by the Executive Council (EC). The new LCCDs were to be formed by nationwide elections. These elections (17-18 July 1985) were the first free and democratic elections to take place in North Yemen. Typically, one elected member stood for an electorate of 500 people. These representatives were also to become members of the People's General Congress. Al-Saiidi explains that the politicizing of the LCCDs was detrimental. Issues of local development became confused with political issues. In addition, other problems emerged, such as the misuse of LCCDs funds, lack of technical supervision, and worst of all, the lack of clearly defined rights and responsibilities of the LCCDs [Al-Saiidi, 1992, p. 58]. Thus, LCCDs represented democratic organizations that lacked any real power to plan, generate or administer projects without the firm control of the state executive power. "Decision-making powers were placed almost exclusively into the hands of the governors, all appointed by the central government without requesting participation at the local level" [ibid., p. 60]. Thus, what had been a grassroots organization of communal development, instrumental in promoting citizen participation at different levels of society, lost its momentum.

In the South, there were various organizations and institutions established to link the central government with the citizens, and that incorporated people's participation at different levels.[25] However, it was the People's Defense Committee (PDC) which was established in 1973, on the Cuban model, which represented neighbourhood group organizations. The PDC responsibilities consisted of a wide range of activities, such as the protection of strategic installations against sabotage, the distribution of cards for subsidized foods, and the mediation of family disputes and divorce proceedings. When these problems could not be resolved locally they were taken to the relevant authorities. Lackner [1985, p. 101] explains that for a long time the PDCs' security function in Aden affected their image and they were regarded by many as a surveillance organization. However, by the early 1980s, their increased cultural and community activities helped alter their image and they became more popular. In the villages, they became successful in forming a local community administration.

Post unification, the ROY government unified the Local Councils of the YAR and the PDRY. Law No. 52 of 1991 emphasized the binding of the Local Councils with the policies declared by government. However, Local Councils have not revived local public interest and participation as in earlier days, since the Councils continue to be perceived as government-controlled institutions.

The ability of citizens — individually or collectively — to voice their demands and needs to government is often difficult and complicated. The problem can be attributed to the following reasons. First, unofficial channels and networks have become more of a norm for citizens to process government-related activities or have access to government officials. Second, a significant number of government employees do not seem to function according to their roles as "civil servants" with responsibilities that are a "public service". Some of these civil servants work in the public sector

---

[25] For example, the People's Councils were organized by the State to represent a system of local government at the provincial level (as discussed in Chapter II).

basically because in the 1970s and 1980s it was the biggest employment agency; while other civil servants are merely interested in enhancing their own political image. As a result, poor and disadvantaged citizens who lack social networks are overwhelmed by what is involved in interacting with their government, and often give up what is within their social rights. Although these rights may be protected by the State, the poor and disadvantaged people are confronted by too many obstacles as a consequence of the lack of mediating institutions and agencies. This problem is not unique to Yemen, but is a prevalent ailment in many developing countries.

Exclusion from representation, therefore, compounds the other new dimensions of exclusion, access to basic services and to the labour market. This fosters feelings of insecurity and vulnerability among poor groups and pushes them to the periphery of society.

## Chapter 4

## *Excluded groups in Yemen*

In the preceding chapters, the concept of social exclusion was explained in relation to the functions of the economic, political, and social systems and the changing nature of social integration in Yemen. The functions of these systems and their relationships with society were examined to define overall processes of inclusion and exclusion. This also involved describing the social strata in the traditional social order and defining the most prevalent new dimensions of exclusion in Yemen — exclusion from basic needs, exclusion from the labour market, and exclusion from social and political representation.

This chapter examines how social exclusion at the macro-level is transposed to the individual or group level, i.e. the micro level. It deals with the way in which certain factors make individuals vulnerable to processes of exclusion relating to the social order or to national development policies. These processes are founded on the interaction between the dimensions of exclusion prevalent in the country, and the underlying attributes, such as social identity, of individuals who seek inclusion in relation to these dimensions.

## *I.  Identification of excluded groups*

The chapter identifies groups in society that may be considered excluded and discusses aspects of their economic and social situation. This task is complex because of the lack of data on poverty, employment, and social integration. For example, there have been no studies conducted in Yemen on poverty (such as those typically conducted by the World Bank), and therefore there is no measurement of the poverty line in Yemen. Only basic data are available on employment. No data are available on employment in the informal sector, which employs a large number of individuals.

Nor can income inequality be explained, again because of the unavailability of such data. Thus, there are no measurable criteria to use in the selection process of the target population.

As a result, identification of excluded groups was based on preliminary analysis of data collected by the author during a visit to Yemen in November 1993. During this visit, several interviews were conducted with officials and representatives in different ministries (the Ministry of Planning and Development, the Ministry of Insurance and Social Services, Ministry of Labour, Ministry of Education, Ministry of Health, Ministry of Agriculture), international organizations, and NGOs (local and foreign). During these interviews information was solicited on which groups they considered excluded in society. Specifically, the focus was on the following three questions: which groups in society they considered encounter barriers in attaining access to basic services, which groups encounter barriers in the labour market, and which groups appear to have marginal participation and representation in society? The author also visited different neighbourhoods that obviously consisted of the poorest groups. However, since poverty is becoming more prevalent in Yemen, it was very important to be able to differentiate between those who are "poor" and those who are "excluded". Furthermore, applying the concept of "excluded" at a more individual level is a sensitive procedure, since this issue, unlike the issue of poverty, relates not only to low levels of income and consumption, but also questions the individual's position in society in relation to social membership. This includes membership at the group or community level and at the national level. Furthermore, it involves the way in which this membership, or lack of it, affects access to goods and services, employment, safety nets, and entitlements.

Another important factor in the selection of the target population was representation from both the southern and northern governorates, since unification was only in its fourth year, and the political economies and social policies of the two states were very different before unification.

Based on the analysis of the data collected during the preliminary visit, the author selected the following four groups: (1) an ethnic minority group — the *akhdam*, (2) day labourers; (3) inhabitants in remote villages; and (4) emigrant returnees of the Gulf War. These groups were identified on the basis that they seemed to be from the poorest groups in society, suffered from lack of access to the labour market, and did not seem to be in the social mainstream. It was also of considerable interest to find that the excluded groups were the same in the northern and southern governorates despite their political history and economic and social differences prior to unification. This does not imply that these are the only excluded groups in

Yemen.[24] Rather, in a first study to be conducted on social exclusion these four groups are significant representatives.

## II.  Overview of the excluded groups

### 1.  Ethnic minority group: the akhdam

The term *akhdam* is used commonly to describe this ethnic minority group in Yemen. The continuing use of *akhdam*, the plural for *khadem*, which means servant, is clearly discriminatory. Its use in this study is dictated by the lack of an alternative way to identify this group. No one is sure of the *akhdams'* origins. They have been described as the poorest and most marginal group in Yemeni society [Shaher, 1991; Othman, 1978; Globovaskaya, 1981; Al-Sharjaby, 1986].

The physical features of the *akhdam* are similar to those of Africans. There have been numerous unconfirmed studies that attempted to establish a link between the *akhdam* and the Africans. The language of the *akhdam* and their religious practices, however, are the same as the rest of the Yemeni society.

There are different hypotheses concerning the origins of the *akhdam*. The first suggests that the *akhdam* were discriminated against in Yemen since pre-Islamic times. There is little support of this hypothesis. In particular, there is no mention of the *akhdam* in the *Hadith* (in the *Quran*) that would confirm their presence in southern Arabia at that time. The second hypothesis is that they are the descendants of slaves. However, historical facts relating to slavery in Yemen do not support this hypothesis either. It is argued that slaves in Yemen, although not free, had more privileges than the *akhdam* and were considered to have a higher social status [Al-Sharjaby, 1986, p. 261]. Another hypothesis is that the *akhdam* are descendants of the Ethiopian invaders who stayed behind in Yemen. Shaher [1991, p. 236], who favours this view, suggests that after the Yemenis overthrew the Ethiopian invaders during the sixth century, they retaliated by making the Ethiopians who were left behind in Yemen their servants.[25] A final hypothesis is that the *akhdam* were originally people of

---

[24] For example, the Bedouins, who were not included in this study, may provide an interesting group for consideration in the future.

[25] This hypothesis is based on the first study of the *akhdam* conducted by Arnaud and Vayssiere in 1850 (translated by Othman, 1978). Studies which followed a century later continue to use Arnaud's study as a main reference.

Yemeni descent who migrated to Ethiopia before the spread of Islam and resided there and mixed with the local population [Othman, 1978]. They later returned to Yemen with the Ethiopian invasion in 525 AD. Some believe this to be a more likely explanation. This hypothesis that has also not been confirmed by others implies that the *akhdam* are an indigenous minority group rather than an out group ethnic minority.

## A.  Social status of the akhdam

There is no data on the *akhdam* that provides information on their demographics (total numbers, their distribution between rural and urban areas, their age distribution, etc.). It is widely believed that the majority are illiterate.

As mentioned earlier, social status in Yemen is based on genealogy. Since the origin of the *akhdam* cannot be traced, their social status can only be based on their occupation. Bujra explains that in traditional times, people divided economic activities into two categories: "respectable and dignified" occupations such as farming or "lowly and undignified" occupations such as butchers and waste collectors. The *akhdams'* social status is based on their involvement in the latter type of economic occupations [Bujra, 1971].

The *akhdam* tend to keep to themselves since they know they would not be welcome if they tried to mix with others in society. They live in closed ghettos of tin huts with no piped water, sanitation facilities, or sewage systems. Their children are frequently not sent to school since they cannot afford school expenses. In addition, children may be called upon to participate in work that will add to the family's income. Those who go to school in some cases drop out as a result of discriminatory practices. The racial and emotional uneasiness and uncertainty in dealing with the *akhdam* is best characterized as "aversive racism". Hagendoorn [1993, pp. 26-51] explains this as a more hidden form of racism which is expressed in simple avoidance. Social distance is maintained, separating this minority group from the rest of society in relation to work, neighbourhood, friendships and marriage.

## B.  Economic activities

In a study of the different social groups in North Yemen, Al-Sharjaby [1986, pp. 274-276] notes that the *akhdam* residing in rural areas are economically better off than those residing in urban areas. In rural villages, a *khadem* is considered a servant of the village. The villagers, in return, are responsible for his livelihood. For example, some landowners would provide a *khadem* and his family with enough crops to last them for a whole year. In some villages, the landowners would allow the *akhdam* to pick crops for themselves. Other landowners would designate the harvest of a small area of land for the *akhdam* workers.

The economic participation of the *akhdam* is open and flexible. In other words, their employment is balanced with the needs of the economy. It expands at times of prosperity and contracts during times of depression. This is especially true for the manual labourers and servants. This makes the unskilled *akhdam* a mobile group that constantly migrate to different towns in search of work. Politically, they are weak and subservient for several reasons. First, they are made up of small and scattered groups. As a result of the lack of stability in their occupations, they always segment and disperse before they reach an optimum size in any particular location. Second, in times of drought or other hardships, they are the first to become redundant. Their economic dependence has always put them in a status of clientship. In addition, they may have 50 leaders instead of a single leader, each heading his own small group [Bujra, 1971, p. 43].

Globovaskaya [1981, p. 183] explains that the *akhdam* in the north are not allowed to live inside the village but rather in small huts on the outskirts. They are landless and their relationship with the villagers is strictly that of an employee and an employer.[26] The number of *akhdam* hired as peasant labourers is also usually kept to a minimum. This is intended to prevent them from entering productive modes of employment in order to maintain their status as servants [Al-Sharjaby, 1986, p. 27]. As a result, they continue to be subservient to the villagers. The *akhdam* in villages work in menial jobs such as butchers, barbers, entertainers, collectors of waste, domestic servants, and hide dyers. In urban areas, these jobs (with the exception of waste collectors) are performed by other Yemeni workers. However, these other workers who also belong to a low social class are not socially excluded as a result of their occupations. Furthermore, the *akhdam* hired to work on the farms are not always paid in cash. They are given crops, food, or temporary housing without having a say in how they get paid. Hence, although more *akhdam* are being hired in rural areas, their economic participation continues to be marginal due to restrictions imposed on their economic well-being.

In recent years, with the high rate of emigration from rural villages and the transition from a subsistence economy to a market economy, more *akhdam* are being hired to work in the land. Globovaskaya [1981, p. 35],

---

[26] During our field visits, we observed that the *akhdam* lived inside the villages we visited. However, there was an obvious segregation between the location and the type of their homes and the other village inhabitants.

however, explains that the *akhdam* are only allowed to participate in the farming of certain vegetables such as garlic, onions, and carrots. These are cash crops that are easily farmed all year round and are considered the farming products of the poor. In a more recent study, Al-Sharjaby [1986, p. 277] found that in a small village in the Governorate of Taiz, this minority group had achieved upward social mobility over the last 40 years. This was a result of working for several years on the same farm, which eventually leads to the landowner giving the *khadem* a plot of land to be responsible for. Gradually this land is legally handed over to the *khadem*. The ability to own land and have control over their agricultural production has improved the economic status of the *akhdam* in this village. For example, it has allowed them to own homes similar to those of other villagers. Some *akhdam* have been able to work in other professions in the village such as plumbers, painters, and masons. Al-Sharjaby concludes that this economic improvement paved the way for the social integration of the *akhdam* in this village. It is important to point out that the Governorate of Taiz is the only place among the northern governorates where this minority group has been allowed to own land. Although there is no existing law or official policy which prevents the *akhdam* from owning land, social practices and/or tribal law have precluded this privilege. The Agrarian Reform Law (No. 27) of the Socialist regime in the South provided the *akhdam* the opportunity to own land [Deeb, 1986, p. 455]. Nonetheless, the *akhdam* continued to be the poorest as far as land ownership is considered. Bujra [1971, pp. 52-53] describes this situation as one of social patterns that do not change overnight. It takes time for the different groups to re-adjust to the new situations. This process of adjustment entails the ability of groups to manipulate the new structure and make use of the new opportunities as well as to break away from ties of dependence that have been carried over from the past. The ties of economic dependence of the *akhdam* made it difficult for them to re-arrange their relationship with other groups. Furthermore, since they were mostly uneducated, they were at a great disadvantage in the competition under the new system. This is why Bujra [ibid., p. 199] concludes, many *akhdam* in the rural areas of the southern governorates continue to have low-paying jobs such as agricultural labourers, servants, and water carriers.

Policies of the socialist South Yemen lifted other exclusionary practices. First, the term *khadem/akhdam* was forbidden since it referred to a social status. The *akhdam* were encouraged to seek education and training. Most importantly, they were given equal employment opportunities. By the 1980s, some of the *akhdam* in Aden were employed in different administrative positions such as civil servants, teachers, policemen, and soldiers.

In urban areas of the northern governorates, the economic livelihood of the *akhdam* remains more desperate since they have no reliable source of income. They live in *mahwas*, which are similar to slum ghettos, consisting of shack houses constructed from wood planks and tin roofs. They work in menial jobs, primarily as the city's sanitation cleaners. It is widely assumed that many of them are also panhandlers. However, a recent study found that the *akhdam* do not represent a significant fraction of the 375 street panhandlers surveyed [Zouby & Hamad, 1994].

During the construction boom of the 1980s in North Yemen, there was a strong demand for unskilled manual labourers. The *akhdam*, along with other poor unemployed men, were hired as cheap labourers. This, perhaps, was an opportunity for the *akhdam* to participate in the labour force side by side with other Yemenis. Ghaleb [1970, p. 35] states that the transformation of society from a traditional economy to a modern economy will lead to changes in labour opportunities and relationships. This may gradually lead to the integration and improvement of the economic well-being of the *akhdam*. However, the economic recession of the 1990s in Yemen has completely eliminated these opportunities. Thus, as Bujra explained earlier, the economic participation of the *akhdam* is always the first to become redundant during a decline in the economy.

Thus, in both urban and rural areas, the exclusion of the *akhdam* has been widely prevalent, particularly in the northern governorates. The *akhdam*, in response, have isolated themselves even further. Most researchers are unable to explain why the exclusion of the *akhdam* has been carried on from one generation to another; they believe that this is not based on racial discrimination. There are other Yemenis of African descent, including descendants of slaves, that are fully integrated in Yemeni society [Al-Sharjaby, 1986, p. 267]. Furthermore, in a traditional Islamic society like Yemen in which all people should be treated as equals, there should be no tolerance of racial discrimination. Nonetheless, social and economic exclusion of the *akhdam* seems to continue as a hereditary trait.

## 2. Day labourers

Day labourers in Yemen are referred to as *al-mouhamashine*, or the marginalized. In general, the term *mouhamashine* could refer to any under class group in Yemeni society. Recently, this term has been widely used to describe poor casual labourers who seek work on a daily basis and gather in several locations in the major cities, especially Sana'a and Aden. They are primarily landless workers and marginal landowners who migrate to the cities with expectations of improving their economic status. Instead, they arrive in urban centres that are poorly prepared to absorb them. Until this study, very little information has been known about this group.

Day labourers first became noticeable towards the end of the 1980s. There are several factors that may have contributed to the increasing numbers of day labourers. First, conventional development planning which resulted in a mal-distribution of employment opportunities. That is, industries, services, and utilities were concentrated in the major cities and their outskirts. This led to a stagnation of the productive capability of the rural population. This, in turn, led to an increase in rural urban migration. The MPD [1991, p. 100] argues that this was not so much a reflection of urban prosperity and industrial development but rather of the deteriorating living conditions in the countryside. The large numbers coming from rural areas to urban centres could not find enough job opportunities. This resulted in high levels of unemployment and underemployment. Consequently, these rural migrants arrived in urban centres that were unable to absorb them and had no existing social networks that could sustain them. A second factor that contributed to the increase in the numbers of day labourers is the high population growth, especially in the 15-65 age group (44 per cent), and the high illiteracy rate among this group. Third, the sudden return of emigrant workers from the Arab oil states as a result of the Gulf War crisis, created a surplus of unskilled and semi-skilled workers. Fourth, the high costs of agricultural production and the low output has led many farmers to abandon their land and migrate to the cities in search of work. Finally, in the more affluent farms, the increasing use of modern technology in farming may have resulted in loss of jobs among peasants that forced them to migrate to the city. However, with the existing glut of manual labourers, they have very little chance of finding permanent jobs in the cities. Thus, day labourers who have been squeezed out from the traditional market do not have the skills to integrate into the new market economy. Hence, the transformation process, which includes changes in the economy and the characteristics of the labour force, are important underlying mechanisms that contribute to the marginal economic participation of day labourers.

Unfortunately, there are no rehabilitation programmes that provide training to these men to assist them to enter the labour market. Poor landless men have more limited access to training in income-generating skills than poor women. There has recently been a strong emphasis on women in development in Yemen, with particular emphasis on poor women. Poor men have been largely overlooked in the process.

## 3. Inhabitants of remote villages

The definition of remote villages encompasses all places a few miles distant from the main road network of the country. Major characteristics of these villages include problems of high emigration, no productive investment, no communication and transportation network facilities. The people in these villages live in impoverished conditions and believe that the Government is not interested in including them in the overall social and economic development of the country. The Government, however, has always considered the social integration of these villages a major priority. The provision of basic services to these villages that are geographically distant, scattered, and where traditional social structures still predominate is a complex and costly endeavour. Thus, the exclusion of inhabitants of remote villages is associated with territorial exclusion.

Disparities in the social services provided in rural and urban areas are best illustrated in the statistics of the Centre for Statistical Organization [CSO, 1991, p. 109]. For example, the illiteracy rate in rural areas is 77 per cent compared to 47 per cent in urban areas. Forty one per cent of primary school age children in rural areas do not have access to formal education. There are 36 urban hospitals and 21 rural hospitals in Yemen. These numbers, however, may give the false impression that health care is readily available throughout the country. There are 5,331 hospital beds in urban areas compared to 1,491 beds in rural areas where the majority of the population reside [ibid., p. 110]. Furthermore, hospitals in rural areas are for the most part primary care providers. Patients with serious health ailments must go to urban areas for treatment. Hospitals in the rural areas are difficult to reach due to lack of paved roads and the long distances that separate the rural population from the rural hospitals, while hospitals in urban areas are easily accessible. Urban hospitals receive more resources than those in rural areas in the form of modern medical equipment, laboratory equipment, and various supplies.

The livelihood of inhabitants in remote villages is also restricted. Agriculture is the predominant employment sector (62 per cent). In the past few years, the Ministry of Planning and Development [ibid., pp. 110, 113-114] reported a reduction in the land cultivated annually. This has been attributed to meagre water supply, migration to urban areas or abroad, limited availability of production inputs, and rising production costs.

Traditional social structures also have had a significant impact on the exclusion of remote villages. In the northern governorates, the social structure is based on the tribal system. Many of these tribal villages, particularly those in the highlands, have been independent of the central government for centuries. The early 1970s, the new Republican government declared that its primary objective was the social and economic development of the entire country as its primary policy objective. This was in part an effort to establish its legitimacy. Major emphasis was placed on improving the living conditions of the entire population by providing educational opportunities, health services, and a higher standard of living. McCohen et al. [1981] explain that, for the rural population, this meant paved roads and water supply to increase their agricultural productivity. Peterson [1982, pp. 116-118] suggests that the State believed that providing rural villages with development projects and other basic services would undermine tribal loyalties and result in the integration of the country under the central authority. Another state initiative was to recruit males from rural villages into the army. Powerful tribal *shaykhs* were also asked to participate in the government. This strategy was most effective in the rural villages of the powerful tribes. Development was not given high priority in the more remote areas with poorer tribes. Instead, priority was given to villages with a high per centage of cultivation and that would be a better investment for high economic returns. In addition, the modest political influence of the *shaykhs* of these remote villages did not allow them to lobby effectively for development projects.

In the southern governorates, the marginalizing of the remote villages was different due to the influence of British colonialism and the socialist regime that followed. Stookey [1982, pp. 75-76] explains that Aden's countryside was marginally involved in the burgeoning economic expansion of the British era. The economic interests of the British in the rural areas was limited to ensuring the security of the caravan routes by which the North Yemeni coffee and other exportable commodities were carried to Aden and keeping the transit tolls exacted by the ruling chiefs along these routes at a reasonable level. The political fragmentation and civil unrest in the countryside also thwarted all efforts to expand agricultural production. Furthermore, the ruling chiefs in the protectorates of Aden were not "development minded".

In the final years of British rule, severe drought and widespread starvation in the countryside forced the British to take vigorous action to expand and modernize the economic base of the country, i.e. agriculture. In one particular region, Abyan, the introduction of gravel roads, modern housing, running water, and electric power resulted in increased prosperity. However, no benefits were realized by the nomadic herdsmen and the peasants tilling tiny plots in the uplands. Stookey suggests that the development directed and largely financed by the British was also accompanied by some social dislocation and political unrest. In some of the more primitive areas, it actually deprived some citizens of their age-old sources of livelihood. For example, along the mountainous routes from North Yemen to Hadramawt to the Gulf of Aden, caravans had customarily employed guides from the tribes along the way and paid them transit dues. Many tribesmen lived by raising camels and leasing them for transport. Small entrepreneurs, principally from Aden, began to introduce the carriage of freight by truck and sought to avoid payment to the tribes en route. The British authorities attempted to solve the situation by forbidding the carriage of certain commodities by motor vehicles while tolerating the collection of tolls. Trucking nevertheless flourished. This, however, gave rise to civil disobedience and banditry on the roads [ibid., pp. 79-80].

Stookey [1982, p. 80] and Deeb [1986, p. 454] both suggest that the inequities among the population, especially the impoverished peasantry, may have contributed to the triumph of the revolutionary economic policies based on a Marxist ideology. The new regime's ideology promoted equality among citizens and emphasized the need to provide the poor villages with basic services.

Following unification, the new ROY government's focus shifted from including remote villages in social and economic development to the integration of the economic, social, and institutional systems of the two countries. The economic recession that shortly followed once again marginalized the remote villages. The continuing exclusion of some villages from social and economic development is increasing the disparities between the rural and urban population, compounding the problem of rural/urban migration, and impeding the transformation of the economy from a subsistence to a market economy.

## 4. The returnee emigrants of the Gulf War

Six months after Yemen's unification (20 May 1990), the Gulf War started with the Iraqi invasion of Kuwait. As a result, of the ROY government's neutral political stance in the Gulf war, over one million Yemeni emigrants in Kuwait, Bahrain, Saudi Arabia, the United Arab Emirates and Iraq were forced home. This represented a population increase of about 8 per cent [CSO, 1991]. The crisis was further compounded by the disruption of normal relations with the international community. The government estimated that Yemen lost US$ 1.7 billion in foreign assistance, oil revenues, foreign trade, and workers' remittances [Stevenson, 1993, p. 21]. The greatest challenge for the Government was to meet the basic needs of the emigrants, who were returning at a rate of 40,000 a day.

A survey by CSO [1990, pp. 17-35] provides some information on the characteristics of these returnees. The majority of the returnees (65 per cent) had been out of the country for over ten years; 10 per cent were born outside Yemen, 61 per cent were born in Saudi Arabia; 75 per cent did not own land/housing in Yemen. Seventy four per cent of the returnees were between the ages of 15 and 45. Almost half were illiterate with only 18 per cent with any formal education; 51 per cent were previously employed as skilled labourers. Most of these returnees did not go back to their villages but settled in the cities. Only 13 per cent had found employment at the time the survey was conducted. These statistics illustrate the difficulties of incorporating the returnees with few skills in an already congested labour market.

The largest group of returnees (92 per cent) had been emigrants in Saudi Arabia. These emigrants were forced to sell their property and possessions at absurdly low prices. To defray some of the cost of providing for the returnees and aid in their resettlement, public sector employees were ordered to contribute the pay of one day per month for three months to a resettlement fund [Stevenson, 1993, pp. 16-17].

Some returnees faced more obstacles to reintegration than others. Those that did not have strong family links in their villages faced the most difficulties. The State provided temporary housing in schools and hospitals. The hardest hit areas were in Hodiedah and Aden. Vacant land was transformed into tent cities. The majority of these returnees, who had limited resources, were confronted with exorbitant rents. They had no place to live other than the state-sponsored camps. Four years later, about 75,000 families of returnee emigrants continue to live in camps on the outskirts of major cities in pathetic conditions. The difficulties of camp life include lack of electricity, uncertain water delivery, lack of privacy, and unpredictable food supply. Malaria and other diseases are widespread in these camps. A report by the Ministry of Insurance and Social Affairs [MOISA, 1991, pp. 4-6] described the social problems that the returnees were facing as a consequence of their unsettled situations. This included outbreaks of fire in the camps, looting, divorce, husbands abandoning their families, high mortality among children and the elderly, and panhandling.

The State pledged to reintegrate the returnee citizens by creating jobs, providing housing, schools, and health centres. The cost of these programmes was estimated at US $245 million. Foreign funds from the World Bank, The German Government, United States Agency for International Development and the United Nations totalled US $60 million. The State made available 60 million Yemeni Rials. The promised programmes never got off the ground [Stevenson, 1993, p. 17].

Unemployment in Yemen between the years 1990 and 1992 increased from 7 per cent to 25 per cent. The crises resulting from the return of these emigrants became a nationwide problem. Shortages and inflation pushed food prices up by more than 200 per cent between 1990 and 1992 [*Yemen Times*, 11 March 1992, p. 6]. Protests and demonstrations erupted in different parts of the country with an increase in frustration due to lack of jobs, inflation, and widespread poverty. In December 1992, thousands of people reportedly participated in looting and burning in Taiz [*Yemen Times*, 16 December 1992, pp.1-2]. Crime was also reported to be on the rise throughout the country.

The returnees' lack of social networks and their depleted financial resources resulted in their being marginalized in their homeland. Furthermore, due to the ongoing political and economic crises in the country, the situation of the returnees is no longer considered an urgent priority. Thus, their exclusion may soon be transformed from a temporary situation to one of a more permanent nature.

## III. Social attributes and processes of exclusion

This overview of the situation of excluded groups suggests that there are underlying attributes of the excluded groups that contribute to their exclusion. For example, emigration is a common denominator among the returnees and the day labourers. The social identity of the *akhdam* similarly is a basic source of their exclusion. Finally, the geographic location of inhabitants in villages seems to impede their integration with the remaining parts of the country. These attributes are associated with development policies and the social order, i.e. processes of exclusion at the macro level. The present section explains the significance of emigration, geographic location, and social identity in Yemeni society, and the association of these attributes with processes of exclusion.

### 1. Emigration

Labour emigration has a long tradition in Yemen. Political instability and economic stagnation are two principal reasons for the emigration of Yemenis from all social strata. However, those from low-income backgrounds are most vulnerable to displacement and marginal livelihood. Their social identities, social ties, and support systems are replaced by precarious living conditions, insecure employment, and an individualistic social existence. Migration results in the separation from traditional productive relationships based on the land, family and community ties. This separation, however, does not always lead to new production relationships. Many of those who separate from the land do not make the connection with a very important condition for the appearance of this production relationship, i.e. productive capital.

Many studies trace Yemeni emigration back to the mid-nineteenth century. The flow of migration at the time was mainly from the north to the south. During British colonialism, large numbers of labourers were needed to build the infrastructure of the city of Aden and its port. This attracted many migrants from the northern and southern hinterlands who gradually became the backbone of the labour force in the South [Wenner, 1991, p. 75]. Many of these emigrants did not remain in Aden. They became seamen who settled in ports of India and Vietnam or in ports of industrialized countries such as in the United Kingdom, France, and the United States [Meyer, 1985, p. 147]. Many Yemenis from the impoverished rural areas of the southern provinces chose to emigrate permanently since they did not believe that their economic well-being would ever improve under British colonialism. Many of these emigrants headed towards the Far East, especially Indonesia. Some became wealthy tradesmen who sent remittances back to their tribes. Other emigrants were just temporary workers from the hinterlands who would go to Aden out of season to work and then return home for the harvest. While these labourers were in Aden, they belonged to the low socio-economic strata within the colonial social hierarchy, even though many of them belonged to tribal class which maintained their high social status back in their village [Lackner, 1985, p. 108].

Migration patterns changed dramatically as a consequence of the political changes that took place in North and South Yemen in the 1960s. In South Yemen, long-term migration increased after the establishment of the socialist regime. In North Yemen, long-term migration decreased after the 1962 Revolution.

The 1970s witnessed a major increase in emigration to the Arab oil countries. Neighbouring countries such as Saudi Arabia, Kuwait, Bahrain, and the United Arab Emirates were experiencing major economic development that was spurred by the vast profits from oil revenues. The major boom in construction in these countries created a great demand for manual labourers. As a result of abundant high wage employment opportunities, short-term migration of Yemenis to neighbouring oil countries increased sharply. At the same time, there was a dramatic decrease in long-term migration [Al-Kasir, 1985, p. 127]. Emigration to Saudi Arabia was particularly easy since Yemenis could obtain a visa at any port of entry without a passport. They also were not required to have a sponsor to be able to work and did not need residence permits. This migration led to serious labour shortages and skill deficit in both North and South Yemen. South Yemen responded by restricting migration after 1973 [Stookey, 1982, p.

89]. In the rural areas of North Yemen, emigration affected virtually every household. The earnings of the roughly 1.25 million emigrants along with heavy foreign aid fuelled the rapid economic development of the 1970's in North Yemen [Meyer, 1985, p. 147].

Al-Kasir [1985, p. 127] describes the main current of migration as one that flowed directly from the countryside to the neighbouring oil-producing countries. Many of the emigrants from the North returned later on to Yemen and settled in the big cities. Thus, going abroad represented a transitional stage between the North Yemeni village and the city. However, by the mid-1980s, this process was short circulated and migrants started moving directly from the village to the city without passing through a foreign country. In this analysis, however, Al-Kasir does not take into account two major events that may have played a role in this migratory process. The first is the international oil glut that resulted in a sharp decline in oil revenues of the neighbouring Arab states. This slowed down development projects in these countries and decreased the demand for imported labour. The second was the ongoing Iran-Iraq war that was being financed by the Arab oil states. This compounded their economic crises even further.

There are opposing views of the impact of emigration on the Yemeni economy. Some, such as Al-Kasir and Stookey, argue that although emigration caused a shortage of labour, a decline in traditional handicrafts, and the abandonment of land, remittances from emigrants contributed to economic activity and the introduction of new craft industries. For example, most of these temporary emigrants who returned to Yemen did not return to their rural villages. Instead, they established small business in the city. Al-Kasir [1985, p. 128], however, emphasizes that these establishments were very small and employed from one to five employees only. Meyer [1985, p. 148], on the other hand, argues that emigration of Yemenis to Arab oil-producing states led to a vigorous influx of capital to North Yemen. Rural areas were the beneficiaries of this new remittance wealth. The majority of emigrant labourers sent money to be invested in house-building, roads, tube wells, generators, tractors, and grain mills in their villages. Many emigrants learned new skills in the host country that were useful when they returned back home. There was a concentrated rise in the yearly inflation rate between 30 and 50 per cent. Prices of imports, particularly consumer goods, increased fifteen-fold between 1973 and 1978. After 1978-79, private cash transfers no longer made up for the continuously increasing deficits in the trade balance.

At the same time, domestic stability was increasing in South Yemen and the socialist regime was becoming more or less accepted. Remittances coming back to South Yemen reached US$180 million by 1977 [Stookey, 1982, p. 188]. This was by far the largest source of foreign exchange in the country. The transfers were accrued by private individuals, usually relatives of the migrant workers. This greatly enhanced South Yemen's ability to import the necessary commodities. The Socialist leaders did not attempt to confiscate these funds for public sector investment because they were aware that this would eventually stop the flow of funds into the country [ibid., p. 189]. Thus, the State aimed to preserve confidence by permitting reconversion to foreign currencies, providing preferential interest rates, allowing duty-free import of accompanied articles, and allowing the funds to be used for construction of owner-occupied housing.

By the mid-1980s, there was a reversal of migration patterns, particularly those of unskilled labourers. The adverse combination of a slow economy (nationally and internationally) and a glut of unskilled labourers led to the marginalization of the new rural emigrants arriving in large cities. The situation was further aggravated by the political events of the 1990s.

## 2.  Geographical location

Factors which influence processes of exclusion can be territorial in nature. In other words, the closer villages are to urban centres, the more likely they are to prosper. Their physical proximity to services and markets enables their inhabitants to participate in economic activities. Villages distant from large town centres, on the other hand, encounter physical, economic and political barriers to economic participation. Subsequently, an exclusionary process is initiated in which distant peripheral villages become increasingly marginalized from economic growth while central villages prosper. This process of exclusion is usually multidimensional in nature including territorial, social, economic, and political exclusion.

The dispersion of the population has been a major obstacle in the development process. According to the National Population Council [NPC, 1993, pp. 3-4], the population is non-uniformly distributed among the 17 governorates (see Table 7). For example, 84 per cent of the population reside in ten of the northern and western governorates (Sana'a, Taiz, Ibb, Laléj, Dhamar, Al-Hodiedah, Al-Mahweit, Hajjah, Al-Baydah, Aden). These governorates make up 22 per cent of the surface area of the country. In five of the other governorates (Abyan, Sa'dah, Hadramawt, Mareb, Shabwah), 15 per cent of the population reside on 58 per cent of the surface area of the country. The remaining two governorates (Al-Jawf and Al-Mahrah), which make up 20 per cent of the surface area, account for only 1 per cent of the population. There are several factors that account for the vast differences in the concentration of the population in different areas.

**Table 7: Population distribution according to governorate, 1990**

| Governorate | Population | % population | % area |
|-------------|-----------:|-------------:|-------:|
| Sana'a | 1 895 441 | 16.8 | 7.2 |
| Aden | 383 601 | 3.4 | 1.3 |
| Lahej | 485 143 | 4.3 | 2.4 |
| Taiz | 1 579 534 | 14.0 | 2.1 |
| Abyan | 304 624 | 2.7 | 4.0 |
| Hodeidah | 1 274 908 | 11.2 | 2.5 |
| Shabwah | 236 930 | 2.1 | 13.7 |
| Ibb | 1 466 709 | 13.0 | 1.2 |
| Hadramawt | 643 096 | 5.7 | 28.8 |
| Dhamar | 778 484 | 7.0 | 1.5 |
| Hajjah | 913 872 | 8.1 | 1.9 |
| Sa'adah | 327 189 | 2.9 | 5.4 |
| Al-Beidah | 383 601 | 3.4 | 1.9 |
| Al-Mahweit | 315 907 | 2.8 | 0.4 |
| Mareb | 124 106 | 1.1 | 5.8 |
| Al Mahra | 90 259 | 0.8 | 12.3 |
| Al-Jawf | 78 977 | 0.7 | 7.6 |
| **Total** | 11 282 379 | 100.0 | 100.0 |

*Source*:    Republic of Yemen National Population Council [1993].

These include climate, soil and landscape, natural resources, and water availability.

A report prepared by the Central Statistical Organization [CSO, 1991, pp. 112-114] attributed the difficulties of economic development in remote villages to the following: shortages of capital investment; low priority of the agricultural sector in national development plans; meagre private sector investment; low levels of technology; labour shortages; lack of basic infrastructure such as roads, storage facilities, energy; problems relating to land ownership. The latter is a reflection of the land tenure system in Yemen. This is characterized by fragmentation into small holdings used for subsistence agriculture. These small holdings produce mainly for family needs only. There is little specialization or geographic concentration of crops and crop price responsiveness. Intensification is not possible because of dependence on family labour and other resources. This land-holding system is frequently beset by conflicts over community rights and tribal disputes over land and water. These complex political and social problems have a negative impact on motivation and are not favourable for increased production.

In contrast, the transformation of agricultural production to suit the needs of a market economy is limited to rural villages closer to major cities. While some of the rural villages in marginal areas were being abandoned, efforts were concentrated on developing the rich lands which have access to water and whose owners are capable of investing in modern agricultural equipment. This intense exploitation of the good land is only possible for farmers who have liquid assets available to them.

An important consequence of the lack of increase in agricultural productivity is an increasing dependence on imports to satisfy the food needs of the country. Growing traditional crops, especially grains, is no longer profitable since the market price is below the cost of production. Hence, these remote villages have been undergoing a process of trans-formation into a marginal productive source.

Another factor that contributes to the marginalization of these remote villages is the highly centralized structure of the Ministry of Planning and Development (MPD). The MPD, which oversees all the development projects of the country, does not always give priority to development projects that are targeted to villages that need them most. This is partly due to the lack of efficient information and management systems. In addition, the lack of technical workers willing to go and work in these areas complicates the development of these villages.

## 3. Structural norms

Access to land and employment are strongly influenced by social identities and networks based on kinship and friendship between equals. These structural norms represent closures which reflect inclusion-exclusion processes. A consequence of this type of exclusion is that individuals whose genealogy is not traceable are marginalized. An individual's economic status by itself is secondary. In the major cities of Yemen, these perceptions are slowly changing with the emergence of a market economy and a consumer-oriented society. Traditional structural norms continue to be dominant among the large rural population. For example, in the villages, social ties continue to be based on family networks and community solidarity. Consequently, those who lack these modes of access encounter barriers to their livelihood.

The dual nature of society reflects the slow transition from a traditional to a market economy. In both cases, there are underlying processes of exclusion embedded in social behaviour. Less than a decade ago, one went to a social gathering and would be seated between a high state official and his driver. In other words, within the social order there was a civic code of respect for the less fortunate. It was also founded on Islamic principles of social equality among all Muslims. Social barriers were conspicuous only in relation to marriages. These types of social interactions are still practised. In the major cities, particularly Sana'a, this civic code has been slowly disintegrating and being substituted with one that reflects a consumer society. That is, social ties are becoming based on economic equals. Subsequently, the social order is being redefined to include those with new wealth, education, and political prestige.

Change in social relations is evident in how people address each other. In the past, during the Imamate regime, regardless of who you were everyone addressed or introduced one another as "brother ..." or "sister...". This expressed social equality. The exception to this rule was when addressing the *akhdam*. The *akhdam* were addressed as a *khadem* or by first name, since no-one wanted to show equality with someone whose origin was unknown. At present, social interactions are commenced by defining one's social position. Inserting a social label before a person's name, such as doctor, professor, minister is the new social protocol.

These changing social relations also reflect changes in economic and political ideologies whereas in the North during the Imamate regime, the social hierarchy reflected political and social power. After the overthrow of that regime, the use of the term *sayyid* was prohibited since it represented the previous social oligarchy. The ideology of the new Republican state was based on social equality and economic development for all Yemenis. In the South, a different strategy was adopted for expressing social equality. The State forbade the use of the term *khadem*. Social equality, in this case, removed social barriers and promoted economic participation to include those at the very bottom of the social hierarchy.

## IV. Survey of excluded groups

### 1. Methodology

Primary data on the excluded groups was collected through formal and informal interviews.[27] Formal interviews were conducted with individuals from the different excluded groups. Informal interviews were also conducted with policy-makers, community leaders, and other social actors to solicit their opinions on this problem. The main objective of this activity was to obtain direct information relating to the issue of exclusion from the identified groups and from policy-makers. For example, how do these groups perceive their barriers to access to participation from social and

---

[27] The research coordinator, Dr. Ibrahim Al-Houthy, and investigators from the Education Research Development Center (ERDC) in Sana'a, participated in the data collection. This included conducting interviews with individuals from the different excluded groups and collecting secondary data.

economic benefits? Do these groups encounter different degrees of exclusion? Have these groups chosen to exclude themselves from society?

Primary data collection took place in urban and rural areas. The three major cities were the capital district of Sana'a, Hodiedah, and Aden. The villages were Wadi Al-Serour (Governorate of al-Hodiedah), and Al-Gawaytha (Governorate of Lahej). Secondary data consisted of government reports and statistics, sociological and anthropological studies, and international social and economic indicators.

The research instrument employed was a questionnaire that we designed and pre-tested.[28] This questionnaire solicited information from the *akhdam*, day labourers, inhabitants of remote villages, and the returnees.

The questionnaire addressed six major issues we considered pertinent to the concept of social exclusion:

(1) *Demographics*: This included general background information such as gender, age, marital status, number of dependents, education, and place of origin.

(2) *Employment and income*: This included information relating to access to the labour market and a livelihood. For example, information was solicited on employment, such as profession, status of employment, income, possession of skills, number of days a person would find work, self employment, barriers to finding work, whether a person would accept any job at all and any pay. Questions were also asked relating to additional sources of income such as property ownership, other family members' contributions, and how they manage when their income is insufficient.

(3) *Living conditions*: This solicited information on housing and the availability of consumer items such as cooking facilities, refrigerator, radio, and television. The rationale for soliciting this information was to assess purchasing power and living styles.

(4) *Access to social services*: This consisted of information on availability of piped water, electricity, health care services, ability to afford medicine, schools, and number of children enrolled in school. In addition, it was asked what barriers, if any, were encountered in having access to these services.

---

[28] The questionnaire was designed by Dr. Al-Houthy and myself. Sections of the questionnaire relating to information on access to goods and services, and living styles were adapted and modified from Townsend [1993].

(5) *Social and political representation*: This solicited information on the availability of a community leader or local council; assistance from a charitable organization, participation in any kind of organization; perceptions of their representatives; and voting in the last elections (1993). Whether they considered it important to have access to any of these organizations or representatives was also solicited.

(6) *People's perception of their role in society*: This solicited information on how people identified their situations, i.e. whether they felt they were part of mainstream society or felt marginalized in society.

Perhaps a fundamental finding the research team experienced during the survey was an understanding of the pragmatic meaning of "social exclusion", by our observations of people existing at the periphery of society. Special arrangements had to be made for each excluded group in the study, in order to conduct the survey. For example, the questionnaire for the *akhdam* had to be reviewed by the Social Organization for Family Development (SOFD), a Yemeni NGO whose work focuses on assisting the *akhdam*. The *akhdam* are very sensitive to issues relating to their role in society, and therefore we needed to make sure that nothing we asked would be considered offensive. The SOFD Director, who is well acquainted with the people in some of the *mahwas* in Sana'a, facilitated our entrance to one of the *mahwas* to conduct the survey since outsiders were not welcomed. She accompanied us to one *mahwa*, introduced us to people there, and then explained to them what our objectives were.[29] If it had not been for the SOFD representatives, we would not have been able to conduct the survey in this *mahwa*. As for the day labourers, the investigators visited special locations in the cities of Sana'a and Aden, where day labourers gathered at specific hours during the day. Our visit to the remote village of Wadi Al-Serour had to be arranged by the Tihama Development Association (TDA), and our visit to the remote village of Al-Gawaytha was arranged by one of the investigators in our team, who belonged to this village. These villages were not easily accessible due to the harsh landscape. Also, since there were no road signs, it would have been very difficult to locate them. The returnee camps, on the other hand, were on what once had been a vacant land 40 km outside the city of Hodeidah. This experience was a strong indication of how these different groups' existence were not within the mainstream of society.

---

[29] Such arrangements were not necessary in interviewing the *akhdam* in Aden.

## 2. Findings

### A. Sample characteristics

The excluded groups consisted of 28 day labourers, 24 *akhdam*, 16 inhabitants from remote villages, and 24 returnees (Table 8).[30] Women represented 26 per cent of the sample population. The large discrepancy in gender is due to the fact that all the day labourers were men. The age range was 16 to 70 years. Eighty per cent of the sample population were married. The average number of dependents per person was six. The sample population was predominantly rural (87 per cent). This study revealed common characteristics among the different excluded groups. For example, the majority are illiterate and unskilled. Most did not have piped water (74 per cent), electricity (59 per cent), a kitchen (68 per cent), stove (85 per cent), refrigerator (91 per cent), television (77 per cent), or radio (77 per cent). Another shared feature is that most men in the sample had emigrated at some point in search of work abroad. These indicators, in addition to what we observed during our field visits, reflect the level of poverty these people live in.[31]

The majority of day labourers in the cities (Sana'a and Aden) are from rural areas (96 per cent). The majority of returnees of the Gulf War are originally rural (91 per cent). More than half of the *akhdam* are from villages (62.5 per cent). These three groups exhibit different patterns of migration. (i) The day labourers engage in temporary rural-urban migration. These men leave their families in their villages and come to the city (Sana'a or Aden) for work. They make frequent trips back to the village to visit their families. (ii) The *akhdam* represent permanent rural urban migration. The migration patterns of the *akhdam* to the city differ between Sana'a and Aden. For example, the *akhdam* in Sana'a are first generation emigrants. In Aden, most of the *akhdam* we interviewed identified themselves as second-generation emigrants. It is interesting to note that most of their parents had emigrated from villages from North Yemen to Aden during the British rule seeking job opportunities that were available at the time. Their emigration was more permanent because they has no land to return to in the

---

[30] The total number of our sample population was 92 people. Analysis of the primary data consisted of univariate and bivariate analysis. Bivariate analysis was performed to provide a more detailed picture of the different dimensions of exclusion each group encounters. Multivariate analysis of this data may be explored in the future. However, it is important to keep in mind that the sample population is relatively small due to the time constraints of this study (N=92). Consequently, this limits the usefulness of multivariate analysis of the available data.

[31] All percentages in the survey findings are rounded numbers.

**Table 8. General characteristics of excluded groups**

| Variable | Number | Per cent |
|---|---|---|
| **Excluded groups** | | |
| Day labourers | 28 | 32 |
| Akhdam | 24 | 26 |
| Inhabitants of remote villages | 16 | 17 |
| Returnees | 24 | 26 |
| **Gender** | | |
| Male | 66 | 72 |
| Female | 26 | 28 |
| **Marital status** | | |
| Single | 12 | 13 |
| Married | 74 | 81 |
| Divorced | 2 | 2 |
| Widowed | 4 | 4 |
| **Origin** | | |
| Urban | 12 | 13 |
| Rural | 79 | 87 |

North and the political situation was relatively more stable in the South. (iii) The returnees, on the other hand, represent permanent migration to oil-rich Arab countries. Analysis of other migration variables revealed that 71 per cent of day labourers, 8 per cent of the *akhdam*, and 19 per cent of inhabitants of remote villages had also emigrated for short periods of time to work in Arab countries, primarily Saudi Arabia. Sixty-three per cent of the day labourers were temporary emigrants, mostly in Saudi Arabia, and had returned to Yemen as a result of the Gulf War. In general, day labourers include returnees and *akhdam*. However, the study sample consisted of only rural/urban migrants. These indicators, in addition to our discussions with this group, suggest that most of the day labourers were rural emigrants who originally emigrated to Saudi Arabia for a few years (one to four years), then returned home for a year or two, then re-emigrated. What differentiates this group from the returnees of the Gulf War is that their emigration patterns are cyclical and temporary. More importantly, when they return, they continue to have strong social ties in their villages. The slow-down in the economy of Saudi Arabia that began during the 1980s decreased the demand for expatriate labourers. This forced rural men to migrate to cities in Yemen in search of work rather than abroad.

## B.  Education and skills

Illiteracy was highest among the *akhdam* (71 per cent) followed by the returnees (63 per cent), and the inhabitants of remote villages (56 per cent). Only 29 per cent of the day labourers were illiterate. Although the day labourers were the most literate, their education consisted mostly of basic reading and writing skills. Most of the day labourers had some professional skill (74 per cent). This is not surprising since most of them had emigrated to work abroad. Previous studies on Yemeni migration have shown that many emigrants learn a skill while they are abroad [Al-Kasir, 1985; Meyer, 1985]. More than half the remote village inhabitants had no skills (63 per cent), mainly because of lack of access to training centres. On the other hand, the *akhdam* with no skills were primarily those in Sana'a since their confinement to menial jobs gave them little opportunity to acquire a skill.

## C.  Employment

Unemployment was high among the returnees (83 per cent) and day labourers (61 per cent) (see Table 9). A relatively large per cent of the *akhdam* and rural inhabitants were employed (58 per cent and 69 per cent, respectively). Their type of employment, however, did not promote social or economic advancement. For example, most of the *akhdam* (men and women) were employed as cleaners in state offices. These types of jobs in the public sector are the most accessible to this group. A few of the *akhdam* interviewed were self-employed. The self-employed *akhdam* were mostly women who were also the primary breadwinners of the family. One woman in Aden made and sold French fries daily in her neighbourhood and another sold candy. A third woman was a dressmaker and a fourth woman, until two years ago, was also a dressmaker. She was unable to continue her work because her sewing machine had broken down and she could not afford to repair it or replace it. This is an interesting case that illustrates how the poor are caught in a vicious cycle from which escape is very difficult.

In remote villages, people's livelihood depends on farming and livestock. The work patterns of people in the two villages in the sample differed considerably. In Wadi Al-Serour, a small village along the Tihama coastline in the northern Governorate of Hodiedah, none of the inhabitants were land owners. They all worked as hired peasants. Their wages varied, i.e. some worked on a partnership basis, others received a daily wage, and the rest were given a portion of the harvest. People from the lowest social class, in this case the *akhdam*, were the most likely to be paid by the latter method. Several men explained that, since their village is close to the Saudi borders, they go to Saudi Arabia to work during the off-harvest season.

**Table 9: Livelihood**

| | Day labourers % | Akhdam % | Remote villagers % | Returnees % | All four groups % |
|---|---|---|---|---|---|
| Employed | 39 | 58 | 69 | 17 | 43 |
| Permanent job | 0 | 33 | 0 | 8 | 11 |
| Income sufficient | 21 | 17 | 31 | 8 | 18 |
| Possession of skill | 74 | 39 | 38 | 46 | 51 |
| Accept any job | 79 | 80 | 25 | 42 | 56 |
| Accept any pay | 88 | 92 | 13 | 38 | 57 |
| Land ownership | 68 | 0 | 31 | 12 | 30 |
| Other source of income | 32 | 38 | 44 | 17 | 32 |
| Emigrated at least once | 71 | 8 | 19 | 100 | 60 |

Most of them make this five-day journey by foot across the desert. There, they work as low-wage casual workers. The money they earn, however, is more valuable back home due to the high exchange rate.

In Al-Gawaytha, a small village two hours away from Aden in the southern Governorate of Lahej, most people worked on their own land. As mentioned earlier, land reform policies during the Socialist years distributed small plots of land to poor peasants. Their agricultural productivity, however, is subsistent and is dependent on sparse rain-fed water supply. Most women in this village did not work, primarily because the land holding was too small and did not need many workers. Some took care of livestock.

The occupations of people in the sample consisted of manual workers (such as construction workers, painters), technical workers (such as electricians, plumbers, craftsman), self-employed, farmers, the military, health care and education (Table 10). All four groups were represented in the manual work category which requires no special skills other than physical endurance. There were no *akhdam* and inhabitants in remote villages represented in the technical professions category. There are several possible explanations for these observations. First, there were no vocational centres in these villages for men to obtain training. They would need to go to a large town or city to find such training. Second, there was no electricity or piped water for such skills to be in demand. Third, their extreme poverty and urgent need of work may be a factor that prevented them from acquiring vocational training. A fourth possible explanation, applicable only to the *akhdam*, is related to discriminatory practices. The *akhdam* are likely to encounter social discrimination in jobs that require some skills, particularly in the northern governorates.

Technical and manual workers consisted of men who were hired only as day labourers. However, there is a difference in the recruitment pattern

**Table 10: Occupation**

|  | Day labourers % | Akhdam % | Remote villagers % | Returnees % | All four groups % |
|---|---|---|---|---|---|
| Farming | 9 | 7 | 58 | 0 | 21 |
| Self-employed | 18 | 29 | 8 | 20 | 19 |
| Manual & construction | 18 | 21 | 17 | 40 | 22 |
| Technical | 45 | 0 | 0 | 40 | 17 |
| Military | 0 | 28 | 0 | 0 | 9 |
| Health & education | 0 | 7 | 17 | 0 | 7 |
| Other | 9 | 7 | 0 | 0 | 5 |

between day labourers in Aden and day labourers in Sana'a.[32] Recruitment of day labourers in Sana'a is the responsibility of the manager or owner of the project who would go to the different locations in the city where day labourers aggregate and randomly select them. In Aden, a contractor would be hired to select a crew of workers for a construction project. These workers become acquainted with the contractor and usually would establish a social relationship with him. Since the contractor has the monopoly of hiring, those he recruits for one project would be given priority in the next. New recruiters would most likely be friends and relatives of the old recruiters. Thus, the exclusion of day labourers from the informal labour market in Aden is primarily a result of lack of social networks.

Very few cases (three individuals) were employed in the health and education sectors. This consisted of a male teacher, a midwife (from the village of Al-Gawaytha), and one female nurse in Sana'a.

In conclusion, the employment data indicates that all four groups have restricted access to higher and more remunerative employment. The barriers to employment that were most frequently identified were lack of qualifications (at least a secondary education) and lack of social networks.

## D.  Income

Data on monthly income showed that inhabitants in remote villages and the returnees had the lowest income among the four groups. The fact that none of the *akhdam* or the returnees had an income above the 4,500 YR bracket suggests that these two groups may encounter more barriers in attaining relatively higher-paying jobs. As for the day labourers, although

---

[32] This was brought to our attention by day labourers who had recently migrated to Aden to search for work.

**Table 11: Monthly income**

| Income in Yemeni rials[1] | Day labourers % | Akhdam % | Remote villagers % | Returnees % | All four groups % |
|---|---|---|---|---|---|
| 0 - 800 | 4 | 32 | 63 | 63 | 37 |
| 801 - 2500 | 39 | 32 | 13 | 29 | 30 |
| 2501 - 4500 | 18 | 37 | 6 | 8 | 17 |
| 4501 - 7000 | 18 | 0 | 12 | 0 | 8 |
| 7001 > | 21 | 0 | 6 | 0 | 8 |

*Note*: [1] In April 1995, the official rate of Yemeni Rial (YR) was $US1 = 25YR. By December 1995, the official rate was increased to US$1 = 50YR, while the market rate had reached US$1 = 150YR.

21 per cent had a monthly income over 7,000 YR, this represents only a very small group. Furthermore, it does not represent a permanent monthly income but rather a consequential income. Overall, the income earned by the majority of individuals from all four groups is very low and indicates their extreme poverty and the economic difficulties they have in providing for their families.

The survey of income included earnings from employment and other sources such as profit from agricultural production, additional income from family members, and others. Information on additional income is important in order to identify safety nets that may be available to the excluded. Most respondents expressed the view that they were not able to survive on income from their employment. Approximately one-third of day labourers (30 per cent) had some additional income from crop production from their land. Also one-third of the *akhdam* (30 per cent) received some financial support from family and relatives. Some inhabitants of the remote villages owned livestock. Some used to receive money from emigrant family in the Gulf States; however, they had lost this source of income after the Gulf War. The *akhdam* women we interviewed in Wadi Al-Serour did not own livestock, they wove straw baskets and sold them to support themselves during the off-season. The returnees were the least likely to have any other source of income. A small minority of returnees (12 per cent) who had additional income had derived it from selling personal belongings. Their jewellery and other valuables had been sold during their first year in the camps. At this stage, they were primarily selling their personal clothing items. Some research investigators made the observation that the quality of clothing of the returnees appeared to be high. This indicates that their livelihood prior to their return to their country was not one of poverty.

## E.   Land ownership

More than half the day labourers in our sample owned land (68 per cent). Rural inhabitants who owned small plots of land (31 per cent) were primarily from the southern governorates. Landless rural inhabitants in the northern governorates were primarily hired seasonal workers who worked for the landlord *shaykh*. The *akhdam* in the sample had no land. Twenty-five per cent of day labourers and 13 per cent of rural inhabitants farmed their land. The two primary reasons given for not farming their land were: (i) their land was too small and therefore not worth farming; and, (ii) the land was not fertile enough for cultivation, especially because of lack of sufficient water supply.

## F.   Living conditions

There were a large number of homeless people among the day labourers (61 per cent), primarily in Aden (Table 12). It is easier for day labourers to find accommodation in inexpensive hostels in Sana'a. We were told that, prior to unification, day labourers were rarely seen in Aden. The Socialist Government provided jobs for almost all citizens. Since the search for daily work in Aden appears to be a more recent phenomena, no affordable facilities exist to accommodate these "new" migrant workers. Furthermore, Aden is known to have a shortage of housing. Some day labourers slept on the beach, while others spent the night on the streets and used cardboard boxes for shelter. Some of the latter told us that, since they had to buy their boxes, it was a problem to find a safe place to hide them during the daytime. The warm climate in Aden all year round made this kind of living slightly tolerable.

During our conversations with day labourers in Aden, we found that the majority were from villages from the northern governorates. They migrate to Aden for temporary work and go back to their villages in between jobs to check on their families and give them money. Apparently, this migratory movement began shortly after the unification. The Government had planned to make Aden the commercial capital of Yemen and re-establish it as a major port as was the case during the British colonial period. Many affluent Yemenis from the north and many emigrants began investing in Aden, mostly in real estate development projects. Thus, these workers saw more opportunity in Aden than in Sana'a. However, it is important to note that this study was conducted shortly before the outbreak of the internal war of May 1994 and thus these migratory patterns may have ceased to exist, since the economic crises in Aden is now more severe.

**Table 12: Housing**

|  | Day labourers % | Akhdam % | Remote villagers % | Returnees % | All four groups % |
|---|---|---|---|---|---|
| Modern building | 0 | 5 | 0 | 0 | 1 |
| Old house | 18 | 19 | 13 | 0 | 13 |
| Tin hut | 0 | 24 | 38 | 71 | 30 |
| Straw/mud hut | 0 | 19 | 44 | 19 | 17 |
| Tent | 0 | 24 | 0 | 5 | 7 |
| Room in back of a store | 21 | 0 | 0 | 0 | 0 |
| Homeless | 61 | 10 | 6 | 6 | 24 |
| **Total** | 100 | 100 | 100 | 100 | 100 |

There was a distinct difference in the housing conditions of the *akhdam* in Sana'a and those in Aden. The *akhdam* in Sana'a live in a *mahwa*. This is a strong indication of their residential segregation. Their homes basically consist of one-room huts made from tin and cardboard. This room is used for almost everything, i.e. visiting, cooking, eating and sleeping. The number of people per room in most cases was nine. Their cooking facilities included a gas burner and some utensils. They had no electricity, sewage and sanitation facilities, toilets, or piped water. They had to buy their own water. A few had a generator for electricity which they used in the evening primarily to watch television. This *mahwa* was also situated near the base of a hill which is used as a garbage dump site. When it rained, the houses of the *akhdam* were flooded by mud and garbage. Since this *mahwa* was located inside the city, it is reasonable to expect that the *akhdam* would have access to public services provided to most households in the city. Obviously, they were deprived of these services. The *akhdam* in Aden, although concentrated in a shanty neighbourhood, lived under relatively better dwelling conditions in cement houses and apartment buildings. On average, their homes consisted of four rooms. This included a separate kitchen and bathroom. They also had electricity and piped water. Some of these homes had stoves and washing machines. We observed that this neighbourhood was also expanding by an extension of tin huts attached to these houses. This suggests that poverty may be increasing among this group.

Inhabitants of remote villages generally lack most modern facilities (Table 13) but living conditions of people in highland villages differs from those who live in villages in the valley. Historically, the climate and terrain were the major factors that influenced the design of the dwellings of these two groups. In the semi-desert climate of the plains, people's homes in Wadi

**Table 13: Access to living conditions**

|  | Day labourers % | Akhdam % | Remote villagers % | Returnees % |
|---|---|---|---|---|
| Electricity | 36 | 21 | 0 | 0 |
| Piped water | 25 | 38 | 0 | 0 |
| Refrigerator | 4 | 37 | 0 | 0 |
| Stove | 18 | 38 | 0 | 21 |
| Radio | 18 | 29 | 44 | 8 |

Al-Serour consisted of straw and mud huts. The size and construction material of these huts reflected the different economic status of each household. A hut is primarily one room which functions as a sitting room, bedroom for the entire family, and a kitchen. Their cooking facilities consisted of a kerosene burner or wood burning. A water reservoir was constructed last year by the *shaykh*. However, this non-drinkable water could only be used for domestic purposes and for irrigation. Women and children, have to walk for at least half an hour to fetch drinking water from a spring. Oil lamps were the only source of night light since they have no electricity. During the rainy seasons, people are always at risk of losing their homes. In the highlands, the villagers in Al-Gawaytha live in old houses built from stone, which resembled caves and not the usual old Yemeni houses. These houses consist of several floors and rooms. Wood burning was the main source of energy for cooking. Electricity was not available. Piped water had reached the village but extension pipes had not yet been installed to reach people's homes.

The returnee emigrants we visited were concentrated in Al-Salakhana, a camp 40 kilometres outside the city of Hodiedah. This camp consisted of cardboard and straw huts and tents. Hodiedah is situated along the Tihama coast and has desert like climate. Temperatures exceed 50°C during the summer months. The dwellings of these returnees provide at best a semi-shelter. They have no water, electricity, sanitation facilities, or privacy. During the seasonal sand storms, their homes are often blown away. Wood burning is used for cooking. Although, our study did not assess food consumption, signs of malnutrition were readily noticeable. People also complained that they could not afford to purchase enough food for their families. Malaria and other disease were widespread in this camp. The living conditions of the returnees were pathetic.

**Table 14: Schooling of children[1]**

|  | Day labourers % | Akhdam % | Remote villagers % | Returnees % | All four groups % |
|---|---|---|---|---|---|
| None | 38 | 29 | 87 | 41 | 46 |
| Some | 0 | 43 | 13 | 27 | 21 |
| All | 24 | 24 | 0 | 32 | 21 |
| Children not at home | 38 | 5 | 0 | 0 | 12 |
| **Total** | 100 | 100 | 100 | 100 | 100 |

*Note*: [1] Includes only people with children.

## G. Access to social provisioning

All groups, with the exception of inhabitants in remote villages, had access to a nearby school. The two remote villages we visited did not have a school. Children had to walk for 35 minutes or more to the nearest school. Whether these villages were in the Tihama plains or the highlands, children were exposed to serious hazards during their trips to school. They did not have appropriate shoes or clothing. For example, children walking under the hot desert sun of the Tihama did not even have hats to protect them from sunstroke. Small items of this nature often overlooked in development may have a significant impact on children's health and educational performance. Eighty seven per cent of inhabitants in villages said that none of their children were enrolled in school. The reason was that the school was too far and the trip was too tiring for the children. The older sons were put to work. Forty-one per cent of the returnees also had none of their children enrolled because they could not afford it. Forty-three per cent of the *akhdam* had some of their children enrolled in schools (Table 14). They, too, said that they could not afford to send their children to school. Expenses such as clothing, notebooks, textbooks, pencils, made schooling unaffordable. One woman who had eight children explained that she sent her children to school by turn. That is, once a child completed primary school she would take him/her out to work and put in the next child.

By comparing the rate of literacy of parents with child enrolment in school, those with the highest rate of illiteracy, such as inhabitants of remote villages, were the most likely to have the highest percentage of children not enrolled in school. In both generations, a primary reason for not enrolling in school was lack of a school and the need to have the children work to increase family income. This demonstrates how poverty and illiteracy are carried on from one generation to the other.

**Table 15: Access to social provisioning**

|  | Day labourers % | Akhdam % | Remote villagers % | Returnees % | All four groups % |
|---|---|---|---|---|---|
| School in vicinity | 82 | 83 | 0 | 92 | 79 |
| Access to health centre | 89 | 73 | 20 | 79 | 71 |
| Can *not* afford medicine | 89 | 96 | 63 | 92 | 87 |
| Encounter barriers to social services | 29 | 39 | 69 | 92 | 55 |

Inhabitants of remote villages (20 per cent) were the most deprived from access to health services (Table 15). People in these villages had to travel for at least one hour to get to the nearest health clinic. The returnees had a small health clinic near the camp which seldom operated (79 per cent). Day labourers and urban *akhdam* have more access to health centres because they live in the cities. Almost everyone we spoke to from all four groups complained about the high cost of medicine. In most cases, they do not even bother to go to a health centre when a member of the family is ill because they cannot afford to buy medicine.

We also asked people if they were encountering barriers to social services. Inhabitants of remote villages considered their barriers were a result of their geographic location. The returnees believed that no-one was concerned to include them as citizens. The *akhdam* felt that their barriers were lack of money to pay for these services. The day labourers felt that the State was not concerned about providing social services to poor people. These reflect some reasons why these groups felt marginalized from social and economic development benefits.

## H.  Social and political participation and effective representation

This data explains political participation and representation at a community level and at a national level. Individuals from all four groups in the sample did not belong to any social or political organizations (such as union, community council, cooperative, etc.) since no such organizations exist in their communities. Fifty-six per cent of the respondents, however, stated that there was a need for some kind of local or community organization. The majority of such responses were from day labourers (72 per cent) and *akhdam* (63 per cent). More than half the inhabitants of remote villages (62 per cent) and returnees (61 per cent) in the sample did not believe that community organizations would provide them with any assistance. Those who expressed a need for community organization believed that such organization might help people find jobs. This was particularly evident in the case of the day labourers (50 per cent). Other respondents believed that a community organization may help them unite and organize as a group in demanding their needs.

Almost all respondents stated that charity organizations are helpful. However, not everyone had access to a charity organization. The majority of the returnees (79 per cent) and half the *akhdam* (52 per cent) were visited once or twice a year by members of a charity organization. These organizations distributed staples such as sugar, flour, and powdered milk. Most day labourers (89 per cent) and all inhabitants of remote villages (100 per cent) did not have access to charity organizations.

Most people stated that their poverty was the major barrier to political participation and effective political representation. They believed that their poverty made them too weak and vulnerable to form any effective organization for political representation. Most groups had some kind of community leader. The day labourers were the only group that had no representatives dealing specifically with labour issues. They had no labour union that could protect their interests. The majority of day labourers were indifferent and cynical about political representatives and their concern for the poor.

Shortly after the returnees arrived in Yemen, they selected their own representative to follow up with the Government on the promises to provide housing, employment, and other social services to help them reintegrate in their country. After many unsuccessful attempts, they had resigned themselves to living with their problems rather than trying to resolve them. At present, their community leader is the *akel* towards whom they harboured feelings of distrust and anger. It was widely agreed that the *akel* in this camp was taking advantage of their situation. For example, the *akel* made those who arrived to the camp at a later date pay him for small plots of land to put up their huts even though the Government had designated this land for the returnees to use free of charge until a solution was found to their housing problem. In addition, the *akel* frequently sold to the people of the camp the food that was donated to them by different charitable organizations!

There were major differences between local political leaders in the remote villages in the northern governorates and the southern governorates. This was due to the continuing practice of polices that preceded unification. In Wadi Al-Serour, in the north, for example, political governance by a landlord *shaykh* was based on the traditional political system. Even though the *shaykh* did not live in the village, he controlled the water supply from the dam and owned all the surrounding farming land. The villagers were economically dependent on the *shaykh* since he was their primary employer. The *akel*, who lived in the village, was the *shaykh*'s deputy. He was the enforcer of the *shaykh*'s authority rather than the representative of the villagers. For example, the *akel* would not represent the people when they expressed their need for a school or access to drinking water. The *akel*'s role usually included resolving disputes among the villagers. If he was unable to resolve such disputes, the *shaykh* would intervene. The inhabitants of Wadi Al-Serour considered themselves isolated from the rest of the country. This was partly due to lack of paved roads and access to basic services and partly due to the *shaykh*'s political and economic dominance. Their poverty intensified their feelings of weakness and dependence.

In Al-Gawaytha, in the south, local political participation and representation consisted of the election of a representative to the People's Defense Council (PDC), organizations established during the Socialist regime. The PDC representatives would present the people's needs and problems during the Council's meeting. Almost every district, whether in the cities or villages of the southern governorate, had a local PDC. Although most respondents did not express feelings of mistrust towards these councils, they did not regard them as very effective.

There is a major difference between political participation and representation of the *akhdam*'s community in Sana'a and Aden. The *akhdam* in Aden are represented by the PDC of the community. In Sana'a, the *akhdam* elect an *akel* from their community as their representative. However, the *akel* they elect merely serves as an arbitrator in their internal community disputes. The *akhdam* in rural areas are under the authority of the *akel* of the village.

There was more political participation at the national level among all four groups. This was reflected by the voting record during the elections of members of Parliament in 1993 (Table 16). These elections were the first of their kind in Yemen, a major initiative of the Government in an effort to promote democracy in the new unified Yemen. A national campaign was mounted to encourage citizens to vote. Candidates also campaigned for months in their respective districts, promising to provide many of the basic needs of the people in their districts such as schools, health care services, water, electricity, and jobs. However, none of these promises were fulfilled in the areas we visited once the candidates took office. This resulted in a strong sense of disappointment among the people. For a while, people believed that their political participation might have an impact on their livelihood. Now they are much more sceptical about political participation and suspicious about the interests of their representatives.

**Table 16: Political participation**

|  | Day labourers % | Akhdam % | Remote villagers % | Returnees % |
|---|---|---|---|---|
| Registered to vote | 67 | 78 | 75 | 83 |
| Voted in last elections | 85 | 89 | 83 | 55 |

**Table 17: Social relations**

|  | Day labourers % | Akhdam % | Remote villagers % | Returnees % |
|---|---|---|---|---|
| Friends in community | 68 | 75 | 31 | 29 |
| Friends helpful | 79 | 72 | 40 | 57 |
| Relatives helpful | 33 | 65 | 40 | 33 |
| Chew *qat* | 82 | 58 | 44 | 58 |
| Attends *qat* gatherings[1] | 58 | 0 | 0 | 0 |
| Difficulty socializing | 65 | 46 | 13 | 33 |

*Note: Qat gatherings are a major means of establishing social networks and information.*

## I. Social ties and relationships

For the *akhdam*, returnees, and inhabitants of remote villages, social relations were primarily limited to relatives and friends from their own socio-economic class. Social ties among them were strong and people depended on each other during hard times. The day labourers, on the other hand, felt that establishing social relations was difficult since they were constantly busy searching for work (Table 17). They socialized mostly with those they met while looking for work or those who lived in the same hostel. Very few of those we interviewed had any relatives in the city. Thus, unlike other rural/urban migrants, day labourers did not have established networks in the city that could help them integrate. Day labourers in Aden believed that they encountered difficulties in establishing social ties. They considered themselves living on the margins of society due to their living conditions. This was compounded by their inability to find permanent employment. Day labourers in Sana'a attributed their lack of social integration to their economic situation.

In spite of the poverty that is shared by all inhabitants of Wadi Al-Serour, traditional social stratification persists. People socialize only during special occasions such as weddings, births, and deaths. However, everyone appeared to be aware of the social affiliation of the others and conscious of the boundaries of their social relations. One woman I interviewed, of *sayyid* origin, was one of the poorest in the village. When I asked about her social relationships with others in the village, she explained that although she has friends in this village, she would not allow her children to marry with them if they were not of *sayyid* origin, regardless of how well off they were. In spite of her poverty, she still considered herself of a higher social stratum. This was something she wanted her children to safeguard. The *akhdam* in this village, on the other hand, were looked down upon and had limited social contact with the rest of the village.

Al-Gawaytha was more socially homogenous since most of the people belonged to the same traditional social stratum. The inhabitants of this village were all relatively poor. Some were slightly better off than others due to additional income received from relatives working in the city or abroad. However, this did not create any social barriers.

The returnees' social relations were confined to the camp. None of the people we spoke to had any acquaintances in the city. They felt they did not have the means to establish social ties with anyone outside the camp. The returnees also felt that since they had been emigrants, they would always be considered outsiders to Yemeni society. They believed that there was no concern among the Yemeni people to help them integrate in their homeland. Many of them considered that their only solution might be to re-emigrate when they got the opportunity.

The *akhdam* in Aden considered themselves poor but not excluded. Most regarded their poverty as the principal barrier to socializing with people from other socio-economic backgrounds. The *akhdam* in Sana'a, on the other hand, expressed a strong sense of exclusion. They socialized only with other *akhdam* in their *mahwa*. The term *khadem* or *akhdam* is seldom heard in Aden. In Sana'a, on the other hand, people are insensitive to its offensive implications. Yemenis in the northern governorates rationalize the *akhdams'* poverty and exclusion as something that they brought upon themselves. They believe that the *akhdam* choose to seclude themselves and live in poverty because they prefer to spend their money on luxury items such as stereos and televisions. Instead of sending their children to school, they encourage them to spend their time in the streets panhandling. The *akhdam* are perceived to have no morals since their women do not wear the traditional veil to cover their faces. Although, integration of the *akhdam* in the south is not complete, it is less common to hear such stereotyping, particularly in Aden.

# Chapter 5

---

# Conclusion

## I. Processes of social exclusion: Macro-micro linkages

The concept of social exclusion in Yemen must be understood as it relates to the notion of social integration. It is a process that denies social membership within the context of a dualistic transitional society. In relation to the traditional society it denies membership in the social order, while in the modern economy state, it denies membership from a citizen's right to equal social participation. The former reflects the dominant social order that continues to determine access and entitlements. The latter reflects national development policies that fail to deliver equal access to development benefits. These processes are not mutually exclusive.

The exclusionary process is transposed to the community level by certain attributes, which make some groups more vulnerable than others. According to the four excluded groups in the study — the *akhdam*, the day labourers, the inhabitants in remote villages, and the returnees — these attributes include emigration, geographic location, and structural norms. These four excluded groups reflect the diversity in processes of exclusion.

The process of exclusion of the *akhdam* is embedded in the lack of social membership in the social order. This process of exclusion is transposed by structural norms, which continue to be practised by society. The *akhdam*'s untraceable social identity impedes their economic and social participation at the community level. The day labourers' processes of exclusion are associated with development policies that fail to integrate this group in the market economy. Emigration promotes the exclusion process of day labourers. In other words, the emigration of day labourers from rural to urban centres, with insufficient skills and lack of social networks, makes this group vulnerable. As a result, day labourers experience peripheral participation in the labour force, and marginal social participation in the cities. The interaction of processes of social exclusion in the dualistic Yemeni society is illustrated in the exclusion process of inhabitants of remote villages and the returnees. The exclusion of inhabitants of remote villages can be explained by national development policies that have not included them in the development process. However, what makes inhabitants of remote villages vulnerable to exclusion is their geographic location. Thus, the more remote the village, the more likely its exclusion from development benefits. Yet the social order also plays a covert role in the process of exclusion of this group, particularly in the northern regions where the social order is more obvious. Thus, if the village is connected to a prestigious tribal clan, this improves its chances of inclusion in development benefits, since tribal *shaykhs* in Government are in influential positions to give priority to the provision of social welfare to their clan. Thus, structural norms, which in this case include patronage and kinship, are secondary factors that influence the exclusion of inhabitants of remote villages. For returnees, on the other hand, the process of exclusion is associated with development policies that have not been sufficiently extended to include their rights of citizenship. It was assumed that their vulnerability to exclusion was related to emigration (in this case immigration), since these returnees were permanent emigrants and had established their livelihoods elsewhere. As a result, this process of exclusion reflected a rupture from one's community and social networks. However, findings from the survey indicated that their exclusion was also related to lack of membership in the social order due to their unknown social identity. This group of returnees had been permanent emigrants; therefore, they no longer had any social ties to a clan or village in Yemen to help them reintegrate. In contrast, other returnees, who were short-term emigrants and had maintained their village links, were quickly taken in by their patronage, and did not need to wait for government assistance.

The most prevalent dimensions of exclusion — basic needs, labour market, and social and political representation — are not mutually exclusive; rather, their interaction leads to a dynamic cycle of poverty, downward mobility, and social exclusion. This reflects the multidimensionality of processes of exclusion at the micro-level. Each excluded group encounters a certain dimension of exclusion, which sets in motion the compound process of exclusion. For example, the day labourers are primarily excluded from the formal labour market. This dimension of exclusion is associated with their exclusion from social and political representation. Their lack of protection in the labour market and insecure livelihood accentuates their poverty, and consequently excludes them from access to basic services as a result of their low purchasing power. The inhabitants in remote villages are primarily excluded from basic needs. Their lack of education and training, as a result of this exclusion, leads to their exclusion from the labour market. Moreover, their exclusion from effective political representation to oversee their provision of development benefits, sustains their exclusion from the development process taking place in the rest of the country. The *akhdam*, on the other hand, are primarily excluded from social and political representation that would help abolish the social stigma attached to them, and confirm their social integration into mainstream society. However, exclusion from representation has also led to their exclusion from access to remunerative jobs in the labour market, and exclusion from basic needs. As for the returnees, when they first arrived they were excluded from basic goods and services while surviving in the camps. Their poverty was made more severe by their exclusion from the labour market due to the degenerative economy, in addition to their diminishing personal funds. The lack of political representation to demand their citizens' rights to assist them to reintegrate into their homeland accentuated their peripheral existence in society.

These dimensions of exclusion are integral to the processes of exclusion. In other words, they not only represent outcomes of exclusion, but also come to reflect the continuation of mechanisms of exclusion that sustain the process. This is observed in the effects of deprivation, which are spilling over to the younger generations. For example, many children are not currently enrolled in school for the same reasons that kept their parents out of schools: lack of financial resources and unavailability of schools. Thus, processes of exclusion can form a vicious cycle that would be very difficult to escape. This problem should be taken very seriously, especially in relation to the high population growth rate among these groups.

The nature of exclusion of each group provides a time profile of the dynamic process that reflects economic, social and political change. For example, the exclusion of the *akhdam* is a hereditary process maintained by structural norms. This process of exclusion appears to be permanent, unless affirmative action is taken by the Government to ensure the integration of the *akhdam* into society. The returnees, on the other hand, are victims of an international political conflict. Their exclusion, however, may have been initiated before the Gulf War. It can be traced back to an earlier generation of people who were excluded from social and economic development. This led to their emigration in search of a better livelihood abroad. Although they succeeded in improving their standard of living elsewhere, a more recent political crisis (the Gulf War) led them to return to their homeland. At present, the situation of the returnees is similar to that of refugees. It is a temporary situation, but one that is fragile under the degenerative economy. Hence, the returnees are a vulnerable group whose exclusion may be transformed into one that is more permanent. Day labourers' exclusion is cyclical. In other words, their exclusion depends on the state of the economy. Yet their exclusion is different from that of the remaining three groups, since they are vulnerable to exclusion only while they are in the cities. Day labourers who maintain links with their villages belong to a community, and have a social base upon their return to their village. The exclusion process of day labourers reflects the serious social calamities in transitional societies as a result of economic transformation and its volatility. The exclusion of inhabitants of remote villages is more complex in nature, since it has been going on for many decades. Historically, in the North this was a result of these villages' weakness as social groups, due to weak tribal affiliation or leadership. In the South, however, it was a result of the subversive policies of the colonial power. Although factors of structural norms continue to have some underlying influence, more recently the process of exclusion of remote villages is associated with the economic constraints of the state and the overall problems in the development of the country.

Other findings from the survey revealed that people considered themselves excluded for different reasons. This also describes at the micro level the way in which excluded groups explained their lack of integration with society. The day labourers in Sana'a and the *akhdam* in Aden considered their poverty the major barrier to social integration. The inhabitants of Al-Gawaytha and Wadi Al-Serour regarded their lack of integration a result of their geographic location and their exclusion from access to basic services. The remaining groups — the *akhdam* in Sana'a, the returnees, and the day labourers — in Aden felt isolated and marginalized from mainstream society. Access to housing appeared to be the underlying factor that contributed to their feelings of exclusion. Housing plays an important role in accentuating the sense of exclusion. Housing is not only a basic need but an important means of providing a sense of belonging and security. It can also be a means of access to work, social participation, and integration. People in more stable housing conditions, such as the *akhdam* in Aden and inhabitants in remote villages, expressed a sense of belonging to a community. Even the day labourers in Sana'a who had been living in the same hostel for many years had established limited social ties with other men in the hostel. There was a sense of camaraderie among them. On the other hand, the *akhdam* in Sana'a, the day labourers in Aden, and the returnees, were living with an underlying sense of insecurity because their homes did not provide them with adequate shelter and were always threatened by natural disaster.

The study also showed a strong relationship between poverty and social exclusion. Poverty and exclusion seem to reinforce each other, regardless of which occurs first. For example, in the case of the returnees, their inability to integrate in their villages was due to a lack of social ties. This led to their exclusion. In addition, their long-term unemployment depleted their savings and made them poor and vulnerable. The day labourers, on the other hand, were poor rural men, whose migration to a new city and inability to participate in the labour market contributed to their exclusion. Among the inhabitants of remote villages and the *akhdam*, poverty and exclusion have always co-existed. At some stage, poverty and exclusion may become indistinguishable. This is perhaps the basis of the common assumption that the poor are also the excluded in low-income societies.

Finally, an important finding is the fact that although poverty and unemployment are prevalent, this did not affect the individual's social ties with his/her family and the immediate community. Family ties were strong and people depended on each other during hardship. People perceived their problem of exclusion and poverty as a problem that involved the family and the community as a whole and not as a problem limited to the individual. This reflects a positive aspect of traditional societies. Unlike Western industrialized societies that have become individualized, where employment is a major determinant for establishing social ties and for social integration, traditional societies' social values based on family and religion maintain the fundamental social bond. This social bond represents a significant "social" safety net that has helped sustain these excluded groups' livelihood.

## II. Policy implications of the concept of social exclusion in the Republic of Yemen

The application of the concept of social exclusion is particularly important for Yemen since social integration is one of the major goals of its development policies. For social integration to be achieved, it is essential to transform determinants that foster processes of exclusion into processes of inclusion. There are several advantages to the incorporation of the concept of social exclusion in the design of development policies and projects that aim to combat poverty, unemployment, and lack of social integration.

The current environment in Yemen is very conducive to the application of this concept since poverty is at an all-time high and resources are at an all-time low. The concept of social exclusion helps to ensure that the most vulnerable groups in society will receive the benefits of development and that their social rights will be protected. It is a useful analytical tool to examine social change and social policies, especially in a developing country in transition. It provides a multidimensional approach to poverty and marginalization in relation to economic, political and social change. The exclusion of the returnees, for example, represents social change as a consequence of political change. The exclusion of day labourers reflects social change as a consequence of economic change. The exclusion of the *akhdam* reflects a social behaviour which continues to be influenced by structural norms. The exclusion of inhabitants of remote villages reflects social policies that are unintentionally widening the gap between rural and urban centres and even between different rural areas. As mentioned earlier, the choice of these four excluded groups was not intended to provide a comprehensive analysis of all the excluded groups in Yemen but rather to serve as examples which illustrate the dynamic forces that give rise to the processes of exclusion of certain social groups.

Development policies and projects can be designed to combat prevalent dimensions and processes of social exclusion in Yemen. For example, as the study of the excluded groups showed, within the dimension of basic needs, education and housing are crucial components for social integration. Although the government has given high priority to education development, more emphasis needs to be placed on targeting the children of poor marginalized groups to make sure that they will be able to complete their schooling. This would provide the means for the younger generation to break out of the cycle of poverty and exclusion. In addition, there are no policies or development projects that focus on the provision of low-income housing for the poor. Yet specific housing policies can be instrumental for social integration since housing gives a feeling of belonging and security. It also establishes the excluded as an integral part of a community. However, for this to be accomplished, the marginal groups in society should be housed within the community rather than at the outskirts of the cities.

Exclusion from the labour market indicates the lack of employment rights and social insurance. This is of particular importance to the large unskilled and semi-skilled active labour force in Yemen. This applies to all four excluded groups in this study. Marginal participation in the labour market emphasizes the need for on-the-job training and the importance of ensuring that Yemeni workers are given priority in the labour market. This includes the enforcement of Article 10 (Employment Law, 1970) which the private sector seems to by-pass. Employment entitlements in the public sector, such as minimum wage and social security, are not applied to such workers. In the private sector, however, according to the Social Security

Corporation (under law No. 26, 1991, cited from MPD [1992]), establishments that employ five or more workers should provide their employees with social insurance. Since this law is very recent, its implementation needs close monitoring. Workers in the informal sector have no protective regulations regarding the work environment, wages or social insurance. There are no labour unions to safeguard the rights of poor casual labourers. Nor is there an adequate welfare system to sustain the poor when the principal provider suddenly loses his/her job.

Social exclusion is propagated by exclusion from social and political representation. Thus, development policies that aim for social integration need to engage social organizations such as NGOs, labour organizations or unions to specifically assist poor marginalized groups in finding employment, receiving training, advancing in their occupations (e.g. from temporary to permanent employment), and overseeing their employment conditions. These organizations would represent a social network that would provide excluded individuals and groups with access to participation and integration.

Social change and the dynamics of social relationships are highlighted by the concept of social exclusion. This is essential information which can be used by policy-makers in their efforts to promote social integration and development. Thus, although society has been undergoing social change as a consequence of the transformation from a traditional to a modern state, this social change has not eliminated structural norms that promote the processes of exclusion. Affirmative social policies that specifically aim to eradicate exclusionary social behaviour will help overcome stigmas and will promote inclusion of socially excluded groups into mainstream society. The success of such social policies was demonstrated by the experience of the *akhdam* in Aden. The state developed specific policies to prevent social discrimination against the *akhdam*. For example, the use of the term *khadem/akhdam* was forbidden. The *akhdams'* integration was catalyzed by education and training, and equal employment opportunities. As a result, the policies of the 1980s, although short-lived, proved successful in freeing the *akhdam* from the social stigma that was attached to them. It also allowed their upward mobility and, most importantly, promoted their social integration. Such policies can also be applied to include the integration of other groups which are vulnerable to structural norms that embody processes of exclusion.

The concept of social exclusion implies evaluating, monitoring and reviewing development policies and strategies. There do not appear to be any policies for human resource development which specifically target poor rural areas that constitute a large portion of the Yemeni population. Current development policies (e.g. rural development designed to increase agricultural productivity) would benefit from a review of their embedded processes of exclusion. A primary objective of this policy is improving the livelihood of holders of small farms and bettering their standard of living through increased production [MPD, 1992, p. 9]. The list of strategies does not include human resource development (such as investment in education and training, provision of health care services or safe drinking water) specifically designed for rural inhabitants. Instead, the emphasis is primarily on the industrialization of agricultural production. In addition, this policy does not include the economic participation of poor landless people in rural areas in order to secure their social rights to development benefits. Poor rural inhabitants, for example, can be included in training programmes for the use of modern agricultural technology and other skills. Alternatively, they may be employed in construction projects to develop the infrastructure of the villages, such as the building of roads, the installation of water systems, and the building of schools and health centres. This would sustain their livelihood in their own villages. Development policies designed regionally rather than centrally can meet the needs and utilize the available local resources more effectively. Private investment in rural areas can also improve the livelihood of rural inhabitants and integrate them in the process of economic development. As a result, this may provide new employment opportunities, reduce rural/urban migration and alleviate urban congestion. A World Bank report [1995] recommends that the government invest in labour-intensive projects, in order to alleviate the problem of the soaring rate of unemployment. Expansion of the country's road network represents an ideal example with obvious multidimensional benefits. It would help integrate all the different regions of the country, i.e. rural/rural, and rural/urban. This would facilitate transportation and communication of markets, services, and ideas. This is a prerequisite for national integration in Yemen.

Other social actors, such as foreign country donors, international organizations, and NGOs, can also benefit from the use of the concept of social exclusion in their development policies and objectives. The application of this concept would assist them in identifying disadvantaged people in society and designing development projects that would meet the needs of these people and make it possible for them to participate equally in society. Foreign development assistance is predicated on the different agendas and priorities of the donor countries. Yemen depends heavily on foreign aid in its programmes of social and economic development. Thus, foreign-sponsored development projects can alleviate processes of exclusion and catalyze a process of integration by means of their development projects. International organizations should take a more responsible role in overseeing that poor marginalized groups in society are included in their development projects. Unfortunately, the international community has in the early 1990s compounded the problem of poverty and exclusion in Yemen by the sudden and drastic decrease in financial assistance in the wake of the Gulf War. These measures, that were intended to penalize the government, exerted their heaviest toll on the poor and vulnerable. The Gulf War demonstrated how development assistance is tied to political objectives that overlook the humanitarian consequences in times of political crises.

Many sceptics will continue to claim that the concept of social exclusion is another discourse of poverty and deprivation in developing countries. As this study explains, poverty and social exclusion are strongly associated. The causal relationship is not uniform in differentiating the independent from the dependent variable. Yet what makes the issue of exclusion an important development issue is that it encompasses the issue of the right of social membership. This membership represents a fundamental human right. Development is not complete when it only provides basic services that would subsequently improve an individual's economic value. Development is complete when all citizens are aware and are able to participate in society, regardless of their identity, religion, or economic status, and when the State oversees and protects these rights.

# Bibliographical references

Al-Attar, M. 1965. *Al-takhaluf al-igtisadi wa al-ijtimai fi al-yaman*, Algeria, Dar Al-Dalia'ah laldiabah wa al-Nashr.

Al-Abiadah, A. 1983. "Modernization of government institutions, 1962-1982", paper presented at the Symposium on Contemporary Yemen Center for Gulf Studies, Exeter University.

Al-Iryani, A. 1992. *Dirasat al-awtha al-maishaah wa al-ijtimayiah la-ahya al-safih bi-amanat al-assimah*, study prepared for the Capital District General Administration Office for Planning and Research in Sana'a, Republic of Yemen.

Al-Kasir, A. 1985. "The impact of emigration on social structure in the Yemen Arab Republic", in Pridham, B.R. (ed.): *Economy, society & culture in contemporary Yemen*, London, Croom Helm.

Al-Saiidi, M. (ed.). 1992. *The cooperative movement of Yemen and issues of development*, New York, The Professors of World Peace Academy.

Al-Sharjaby, G. 1986. *Al-shara'eh al-ijtimayiah al-taglidiyah fi al-moujtama al-yamani*, Beirut, Dar Al-Hadith.

Bujra, A. 1971. *The politics of stratification: A study of political change in a South Arabian town*, Oxford, Clarendon Press.

Center for Statistical Organization (CSO). 1990. *Al-mougtariboun*, Sana'a, Ministry of Planning and Development.

—. 1991. *Population and development in the Yemen ArabRepublic*, Proceedings of the first national population policy conference, Sana'a, Ministry of Planning and Development.

Chaudry, K. 1989. "The price of wealth: Business and state in labour remittance and oil economies", in *International Organization*, Vol. 43, No. 1, Winter, pp. 101-147.

Deeb, M. 1986. "Radical political ideologies and concepts of property in Libya and South Yemen", in *Middle East Journal*, No. 40, pp. 445-461.

Dresch, Paul. 1989. *Tribes, government and history in Yemen*, New York, Clarendon Press.

Economist Intelligence Report (EIU). 1994. *Country report Oman, Yemen, Second Quarter Report*, London, The Economist Intelligence Unit.

—. 1995. *Country profile: Oman, Yemen, 1994-1995*, London, The Economist Intelligence Unit.

Faria, V. 1995. "Social exclusion and Latin American analyses of poverty and deprivation", in Rodgers, G. et al. (eds.): *Social exclusion: Rhetoric, reality, responses*, Geneva, International Institute for Labour Studies.

Ghaleb, M.A. 1970. *Nitham al-hukm wa al-takhaluf al-igtisadi fi al-Yaman*, Beirut, Dar Al-Hana.

Globovaskaya, Elena (translated by M.A. Bahr). 1981. *Hawl masalat al-fiat al-dunya fi al-haykal al-ijtima'i al-yamani*, Sana'a, Dirasaat Yamaniyah, pp. 172-204.

Gore, Charles. 1994. *Social exclusion and Africa: A review of the literature*, Discussion Paper Series No. 62, Geneva, International Institute for Labour Studies.

—. 1995. "Markets, citizenship and social exclusion", in Rodgers, G. et al. (eds.): *Social exclusion: Rhetoric, reality, responses*, Geneva, International Institute for Labour Studies, pp. 103-115.

Gugler, J. (ed.). 1988. *The urbanization of the third world*, Oxford, Oxford University Press.

Hagendoorn, L. 1993. "Ethnic categorization and outgroup exclusion", in *Ethnic and Racial Studies*, Vol. 16, No. 1, pp. 26-51.

Hashem, M.H. 1984. "Political change in Yemen: Legitimacy and modernization", Durham, Duke University, Master's thesis.

—. 1992. "Factors that influence school effectiveness in primary schools in Sana'a", Ann Arbor, University of Michigan microfilms.

Holton, R.J. 1992. *Economy and society*, London, Routledge.

Human Rights Watch Middle East (HRW). 1992. *Yemen — Steps toward civil society*, New York, Human Rights Watch/Middle East, Vol. 4, Issue 10.

Huntington, S. 1965. "Political development and political decay", in *World Politics*, Vol. XVII, No. 31, April, pp. 386-411.

Ismael, T.; Ismael, J. 1986. *The People's Democratic Republic of Yemen: The politics of social transformation*, London, Frances Pinter Publishers.

Lackner, H. 1985. *PDR Yemen: Outpost of socialist development*, London, Ithaca Press.

McCohen, J. et al. 1981. "Development from below: Local development associations in the Yemen Arab Republic", in *World Development*, No. 19, pp. 1039-1061.

Meyer, G. 1985. "Labour emigration and internal migration in the Yemen Arab Republic", in Pridham, B.R. (ed.): *Economy, society and culture in contemporary Yemen*, London, Croom Helm.

Ministry of Education. 1992. *Educational Statistics 1987-1988*, Sana'a, Ministry of Education.

Ministry of Health (MOH). 1994. *Forward-looking strategies and policies for health development in the Republic of Yemen*, Sana'a, Ministry of Health.

Ministry of Insurance and Social Affairs (MOISA). 1991. *Al-mougtaribin*, paper prepared for the Government of the Republic of Yemen.

Ministry of Legal Affairs (MLA). 1991. *The Republic of Yemen, al-Jaridah al-rasmiah*, Sana'a, Ministry of Legal Affairs.

Ministry of Planning and Development of the Republic of Yemen (MPD). 1991. *Population and development*, Sana'a, Ministry of Planning and Development.

—. 1992. *General Economic Memorandum, Round Table Conference*, Geneva, June-July.

Molyneux, M. 1982. *State policies and the position of women workers in the People's Democratic Republic of Yemen, 1967-77*, Geneva, International Labour Organization.

National Population Council (NPC). 1993. "Report of population distribution: Impact and results", Paper presented at the National Seminar for Population Policy, Sana'a, November.

Othman, A.A. (translated). 1978. "Al-akhdam fi al-Yemen: Aslahum wa tagaliedahum"., in *Majalat al-Dirasat al-Yamaniyah*, No. 1, pp. 69-77.

Paugum, S. 1993. *La disqualification sociale, essai sur la nouvelle pauvreté*, Paris, Presses Universitaires de France.

Peterson, J.E. 1982. *Yemen — The search for a modern state*, London, Croom Helm.

Piepenburg, F. 1992. "The coperative movement of Yemen: Developments after 1985", in Al-Saiidi, M. (ed.): *The cooperative movement of Yemen and issues of development*, New York, The Professors of World Peace Academy.

Rodgers, G. 1994. *Overcoming social exclusion: Livelihoods and rights in economic and social development*, Discussion Paper Series No. 72, Geneva, International Institute for Labour Studies.

Shaher, K. 1991. "Al-buniah al-ijtimayiah al-taglidiyah fi al-yaman", in *Dirasaat Yamaniyah*, No. 43, pp. 211-248.

Silver, H. 1995. *Social solidarity and social exclusion: Three paradigms*, Discussion Paper Series No. 69, Geneva, International Institute for Labour Studies.

Stevenson, T. 1993. "Yemeni workers come home, reabsorbing one million migrants", in *Middle East Report*, March-April, pp. 15-20.

Stookey, R.W. 1974. "Social structure and politics in the Yemen Arab Republic", in *Middle East Journal*, Vol. 28, No. 4, pp. 248-260.

—. 1982. *South Yemen: A Marxist republic in Arabia*, Boulder, Westview Press.

Townsend, P. 1993. *The international analysis of poverty*, New York, Harvester Wheatsheaf.

Wenner, M. 1991. *The Yemen Arab Republic: Development and change in an ancient land*, Boulder, Westview Press.

Wolfe, M. 1994. *Some paradoxes of social exclusion*, Discussion Paper Series No. 63, Geneva, International Institute for Labour Studies.

World Bank. 1979. *The People's Democratic Republic of Yemen*, Washington DC, World Bank.

—. 1995. *Republic of Yemen: Dimensions of economic adjustment and structural reform*, Washington, DC, The World Bank, Report No. 14029.

Yepez, I. 1994. *Review of the French and Belgian literature on social exclusion: A Latin American perspective*, Discussion Paper Series No. 71, Geneva, International Institute for Labour Studies.

Zabarah, M. 1982. *Yemen: Traditionalism versus modernity*, New York. Praeger.

—. 1983. "The Yemeni Revolution of 1962 seen as a social revolution", unpublished paper prepared for the Symposium on Conteporary Yemen Center for Gulf Studies, Exeter University.

Zouby, M.; Hamad, N. 1994. *Thahirat tasawul al-adfal fi madinat Sana'a*, Sana'a, Majalat al-Dirasat al-Yamaniah, No. 54.

## LIST OF DISCUSSION PAPERS
## FROM THE IILS/UNDP SOCIAL EXCLUSION PROJECT

*Social exclusion and Africa south of the Sahara: A review of the literature*, by Charles Gore. DP 62, 1994.

*Social exclusion in Latin America: An annotated bibliography*, by Vilmar E. Faria. DP 70, 1994.

*Social exclusion and South Asia*, by Arjan de Haan and Pulin Nayak. DP 77, 1995.

*Social exclusion in the Philippines: A review of literature*, by the Institute for Labor Studies, Philippines. DP 79, 1995.

*Bibliographie de l'exclusion dans les pays arabes du Maghreb et du Machreq*, by Mongi Bédoui. DP 80, 1995.

*The social impact of economic reconstruction in Vietnam: A selected review*, by Do Duc Dinh. DP 81, 1995.

*Social integration policies in Malaysia: A review of literature and empirical material*, by Lim Teck Ghee. DP 82, 1995.

*Policies to combat social exclusion: A French-British comparison*, by Hilary Silver and Frank Wilkinson. DP 83, 1995.

*Evolution de l'approche de la pauvreté par l'Organisation internationale du Travail*, by Maryse Gaudier. DP 85, 1995.

Copies of these discussion papers, as well as the complete list of IILS publications can be obtained upon request from the International Institute for Labour Studies, P. O.Box 6, CH-1211 Geneva 22.

The contribution of the International Institute
for Labour Studies of the ILO
to the World Summit for Social Development

# Social exclusion:
# Rhetoric, reality, responses
Edited by Gerry Rodgers, Charles Gore
and José B. Figueiredo

# The poverty agenda and the ILO:
# Issues for research and action
Edited by Gerry Rodgers

# Reducing poverty through labour
# market policies
Edited by José B. Figueiredo and Zafar Shaheed

# The poverty agenda:
# Trends and policy options
Edited by Gerry Rodgers and Rolph van der Hoeven

# Poverty, inequality, exclusion:
# New approach to theory and practice
Maryse Gaudier

Copies of these titles can be obtained from ILO Publications,
International Labour Office, CH-1211 Geneva 22 (Switzerland).